The Loneliness of a Long Distant Future

ROMI KHOSLA

Dilemmas of Contemporary Architecture

For
Peter Cook
who taught me to invent futures and believe in them

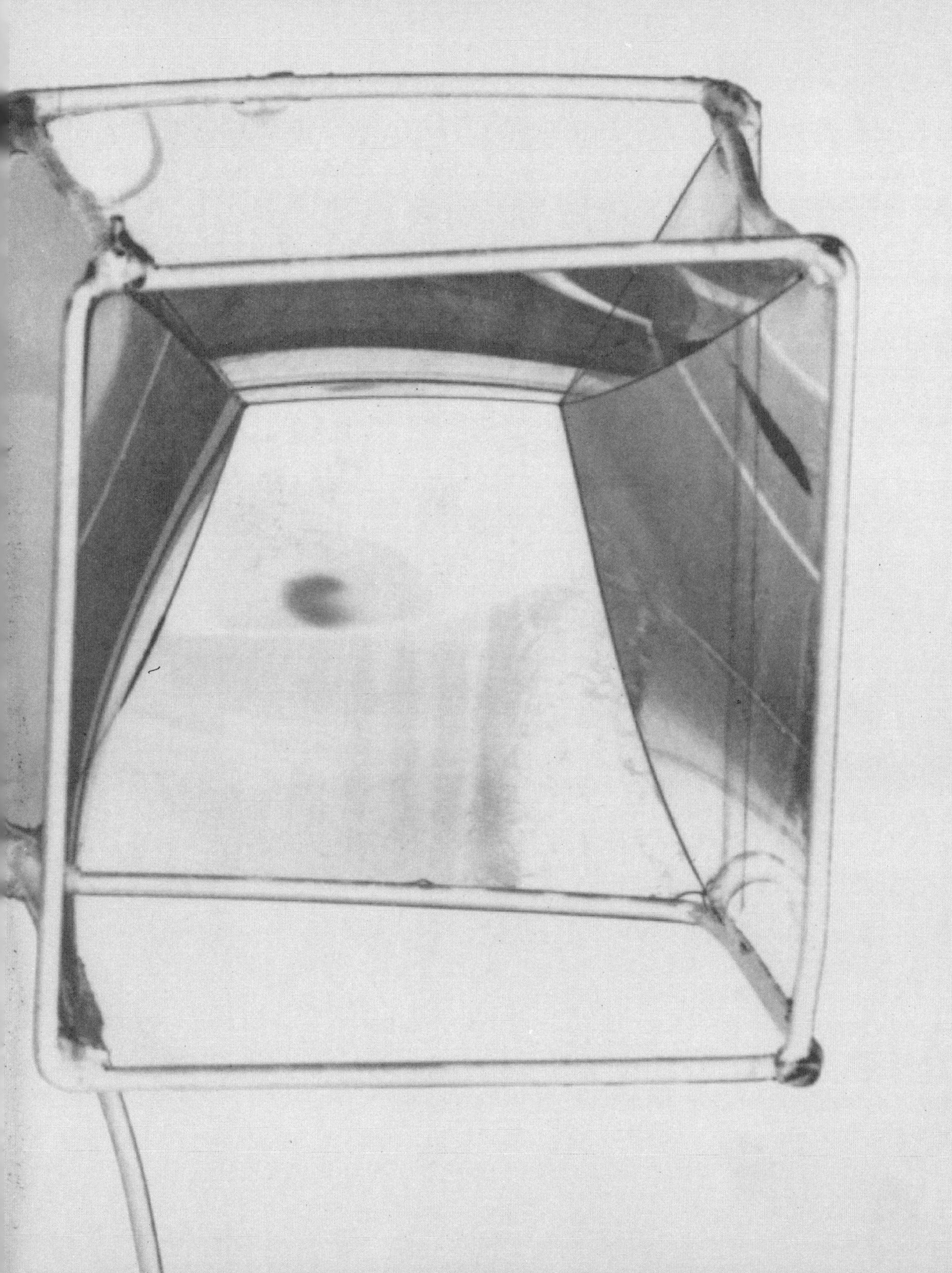

Contents

Introduction One

Prabhat Patnaik

hile reading Romi Khosla's manuscript I was reminded of a remark made to me by a Hungarian filmmaker when I had visited that country a couple of years ago: 'Thank God the twentieth century is over. It was a terrible century!' I had vehemently disagreed with him at the time. India's independence after two hundred years of colonial rule alone was enough to make the century worthwhile for me. Nowadays I would be less vehement, though on balance I would still adhere to my position.

While the century witnessed, according to Khosla, '187 million deaths . . . through human decisions and actions', its achievements have turned out to be less durable than we had imagined. The collapse of the socialist project of course was momentous, but no less so was the other development of the late twentieth century that was closely intertwined with it, namely, the process of 'globalization' under the aegis of the dominant capitalist powers. This, apart from pushing millions into abject poverty, threatens, with apparently increasing success, to reverse the process of 'decolonization' itself. The abrogation of independence of the third world that was started in the economic realm in the eighties and nineties is now being carried to completion in the political realm, especially after September 11, under the 'Bush Doctrine': 'Whoever is not with us is with the terrorists and hence deserves to be so treated.' I would now feel less confident citing India's independence to my Hungarian interlocutor, for the content of that independence has been, and continues to be, whittled down. It is not surprising in this context that 'abstract futures', as Khosla puts it, are no longer on the agenda.

And yet I would not dismiss the achievements of the twentieth century. Taking India as a 'representative sample', at least two phenomena stand out. First, notwithstanding the betrayed promises of independence, notwithstanding the continued existence of the mass poverty that was bequeathed to us by colonialism (poverty in the modern sense, involving insecurity, which is qualitatively different from what existed earlier), there has been a dramatic improvement in the living conditions of the people, including the poor. This has been largely a result of technological breakthroughs, but independence has helped garner the fruits of these breakthroughs for the benefit of the people. In colonial India people 'died like flies' (what else does a life expectancy of twenty-seven years mean?); contemporary India is much better off in comparison.

The second phenomenon is an enormous change both in societal relations and, parallely, in the consciousness of the people. The change in relations has been marked by the acquisition of greater rights by the people, while the change in consciousness has been marked by a greater awareness of rights, a greater desire for freedom, and a rejection of hierarchies and, more generally, of fatalism. It is noteworthy that in India, from one general election to the next, the proportion of the underprivileged – dalits, tribals and women – who exercise their franchise has kept going up even as the middle classes have become increasingly apathetic towards the electoral process.

Khosla uses the term 'ancient futures' to capture the turning of backs to 'modernity' that is currently visible in many third-world societies in the wake of the collapse of 'abstract futures'. But the quest for 'ancient futures' is characterized by two features of significance (*Hindutva* being an exception in both respects): first, its anti-'modernism' is associated with an anti-imperialism; second, it has not sought to usher in feudal class hierarchies (though it has degraded the status of women). The quest for 'ancient futures', in other words, has occurred within a 'modern' context, eschewing what is palpably unacceptable to the people and being contested where it has not (for example, in the case of women).

To put it differently, the twentieth century has been marked by an enormous diffusion of the 'bourgeois revolution' from a few metropolitan countries to far-flung corners of the third world. This fact is so little appreciated that a word on it may be in order.

The notion of the 'bourgeois revolution' that we all have identifies it generally with a replication of the experience of the advanced capitalist countries. And since such replication is not possible both because the historical context is different today and more fundamentally because the success of the 'bourgeois revolution' in the west owed not a little to the subjugation of the third world, the tendency invariably is to debunk the vigour of the (arrested and no doubt potentially circumscribed) 'bourgeois revolution' as is occurring in the third world.

This, however, is erroneous. The fact that this 'bourgeois revolution' has not followed the same trajectory as it did in the metropolitan countries, for example, breaking land-ownership concentration, or the fact that it has not ushered in capitalist industrialization rapid enough for meeting peoples' aspirations or for closing the 'gap' with the advanced countries, or even the fact that the autonomy of the bourgeoisie itself has been undermined by imperialism, causing severe tensions within the 'bourgeois revolution', should not obscure the ubiquity of the 'bourgeois revolution' that has been a feature of the third world in the twentieth century. Indeed, the internal and persistent struggles against fundamentalist regimes underscores this fact. Jurgen Habermas is right in drawing attention to the 'collapse of the utopian energies of the nineteenth century' in recent years, but this collapse has not gone to the point where the people lack the energy to defend their gains in terms of 'bourgeois' rights.

Putting it differently, the collapse of the extant socialist project should not mislead us into believing that the freedom project unleashed by the French Revolution, of which the socialist project constituted a legacy, has also collapsed. Indeed, the collapse of the extant socialist project itself was predicated on the promise of greater freedom. The fact that the ex-socialist countries have taken an altogether different trajectory from that visualized by the protagonists of the change indicates not that the change was not informed by the desire for freedom, but that there were severe constraints imposed by the existing material conditions which always limit the range of possibilities and prevent the spontaneous outcome of peoples' actions from coinciding with their intentions. (The aftermath of the collapse of extant socialism thus vindicates, paradoxically, the truth of Marxism.)

'Modernity', it would follow, is a derived project, derived from the basic project of human freedom. The question that confronts us is: if the socialist project has collapsed and if the reactionary religious fundamentalisms that have sprouted in its place are capable only of stifling rather than carrying forward the project of freedom, then how does the quest for freedom get advanced in the current conjuncture? If there are no 'abstract futures' and if 'ancient futures' are non-starters, then what is to be done? This question constitutes the central concern of Romi Khosla's book. Though it is examined and answered within a discourse relating to architecture, this discourse itself is located within a broader social context.

The specificity of his answer lies in his moving away from an exclusive reliance on the nation-state as the principal agency of change. Whether it was in third-world economies interested in accelerating development in the period after decolonization, or in advanced capitalist economies interested in achieving high levels of activity through Keynesian demand management, or in socialist economies interested in undertaking comprehensive planned development, the post-war period was characterized by a pervasive perception of the nation-state as the agency of intervention on behalf of the people. This role of the nation-state was not confined to the sphere of the economy; it encompassed almost every sphere of social life. The contradiction between an active agency role for the nation-state and the process of globalization which exposes the country to free movement of internationally mobile finance capital, and hence to its caprices, is by now well-known. In the con-text of this contradiction, while the 'neo-liberals' have advocated a withdrawal of the state from any role other than a mere supporter of internationally mobile finance capital, critics of 'neo-liberalism' have argued for a restoration of the agency role of the state by placing controls on the cross-border mobility of finance capital.

While Romi Khosla does not discuss this particular issue, he moves away from the nation-state in two quite different directions. One is his cognizance of the possibility, indeed the necessity in certain circumstances, of 'one state with two nations'. The case cited by him is the Palestine–Israel conflict, where he underscores the importance of water management and water distribution in the region as a whole. Such management must necessarily transcend the boundaries of a particular nation-state. Khosla visualizes a United States of Canaan comprising both Palestine and Israel, towards whose foundation his contribution as a planner is a proposal for a railway-line linking ten stations strewn across the entire region. This proposal is coupled with another ambitious proposal of a water pipe-line. Indeed, his vision is that the railway-line should 'ride over' the water pipe-line which would carry water from the desalination plants on the coast and from the aquifers fed by the drainage from the uplands to the arid regions of the West Bank.

The second break from the nation-state, though expressed by Khosla in the context of museums in his remarkably perceptive essay, 'Museums for Another Future', has an obviously wider significance. He argues:

> The degree of control that the government exercises on them is a direct function of its desire to exert its centralism and authority. The more power and control the government exercises over museums, the more it wants to counter new ideas about culture, and the more it seeks to portray its own version of culture.

This notion of the nation-state as an authority countering creativity points not just to the oft-repeated need for autonomy of the civil society from the leviathan called the state but, more importantly, to a parallel need for decentralizing the structures of the state itself. Khosla, in other words, wants to make the nation-state malleable. On the one hand, he wants to stretch it to cover more than one nation if necessary; on the other hand, he wants it to contract in terms of its centralized jurisdiction by both decentralizing itself and in the process having its extremities dissolved in civil society.

This attractive and essentially dynamic perception has to be distinguished from the somewhat naive view which holds that in the era of globalization, since the nation-state is outmoded, progress in the sense of transcendence of existing structures can come about only through global struggles. This latter view appears to me to be a 'liquidationist' one, while Khosla's is not: its acceptance would entail an abandonment of all struggles for the present (perhaps for ever), since all existing struggles are essentially localized within the nation.

The two innovations relating to the nation-state suggested by Khosla are in turn linked. This link is provided by the 'mesocosmic space' which is his point of architectural intervention, and which is the instrument through which both the expansion and the contraction of the centralized authority is to be effected. 'Macrocosmic space bulldozes and codifies local culture and replaces it with a written macro-moral order.' On the other hand, 'Mesocosmic space carries the evolution of local cultures into the contemporary world without a fear of the modern. Mesocosmic space keeps equidistant fom religious and municipal dictates.' In discussing the mesocosmic space Khosla invokes the notion of 'community'. One wonders if one can draw a parallel here to the notion of *panchayats* in Kerala which, in a universe where egalitarian land reforms have been effected, are also capable of becoming an effective point of intervention, influencing the shape of the nation-state but not negating its existence. Many such questions come to one's mind while going through Khosla's book which, apart fom being an instructive essay on his theoretical journey, gives a fascinating account of his spatial journeys to places like Kosovo and Palestine – places which, though far apart, share the common experience of having been in the eye of the storm. But I must leave the reader to savour the food for thought provided by Khosla.

Introduction Two

Romi Khosla

It is difficult to accept that the challenges of surviving as a collective of civilizations can be met simply by accepting the role that is ascribed to the market mechanism. Somehow its wonderful self-correcting and regulating responsibilities seem outside the realms of accountability. Too many regions on the globe have begun receding into a net of interconnected depressions that have resulted from the constant battering of being 'in transition'. The economic collapse of the socialist countries, the questionable status of the nation-state and the accompanying intensity of armed struggles against centralized authority continue to destroy the certainty of daily life in large areas of the world.

This book is about some of these difficulties and the reasons for not accepting them as being inevitable. The excitement of the beginning of a new millennium seems to be evaporating in the pessimistic scenario that surrounds us. Ignorance about those regions where futures are crumbling prompted me to reactivate some dormant opportunities and go to work in parts of the world where the hopes for a new future had all but disappeared. Four years ago, I disengaged myself from my professional architectural practice and went to work for the United Nations as a principal international consultant. Subsequently, I worked with the national and municipal governments of Palestine, Kosovo, Bulgaria, Romania, Montenegro and Cyprus. In all these countries the work consisted of formulating, establishing and running projects for the attempted recovery of normal life. Some of these projects were implemented successfully, others are up and running, while still others were simply abandoned for being too radical, ambitious or unsuited to the interests of the donor. But, despite the uneven response from national governments and transatlantic financial institutions, it was the process of researching and formulating each project that was extremely valuable for me. Apart from gaining access to gross national data to supplement the research phase, I was able to freely interact directly with the various administrations and citizens as well as travel extensively. The observations in this book are therefore based not on a view through the car-window, but rather on experiences that were gathered through the dozens of journeys that were undertaken during numerous missions in Eastern Europe, the Middle East, Central Asia and China. As the year 2000 began I had already spent eight months working with the Ministry of Education of the Palestinian National Authority. This work overlapped with the conclusion of running two years of employment projects in twelve cities in Bulgaria with the Ministry of Labour and Social Welfare. The employment programme is currently being extended to thirty-three cities in Bulgaria as well as to selected cities in Romania. The prolonged success of this programme contrasts vividly with the abandonment of the projects proposed in Kosovo, where internal rivalries amongst the various United Nations agencies, the incomprehensible attitude of the European Union and the nebulous interests of the World Bank ensured that the reconstruction effort would be spearheaded by the Kosovars using their ingenuity and meagre savings, and not relying on the bickerings of the North Atlantic donor community.

In some ways the chapters in this book can be considered to be a series of interlinked arguments that are made from two simultaneous positions. In one position I am an unknown, helpless and silent observer who has had close encounters and walked through the rubble in the aftermath of the explosions left behind by the terrible events that are still simmering in Palestine and Yugoslavia. As this silent observer I went on a series of missions. During one of these missions, my office in Ramallah was indiscriminately fired on by advancing Israeli troops who were aiming at stone-throwing Palestinian students on the roof. My timely escape a few minutes before the bullets shattered all the windows in the room where I sat was a real reminder of the madness of the times. I am indeed grateful to the Palestinians who hauled me out of my chair and crouched with me behind a parked car. They smiled at my efforts to protect my head with a briefcase full of UN documents. On another occasion, I had to walk around the debris of shelled-out villages in Kosovo holding up the UN identity card chained round my neck in the perpetual hope that this would bring safety from snipers. But the madness always comes through. As I attempted to cross the border into Croatia, local militia soldiers hauled me out of the car at gunpoint and screamed at me to return to Kosovo on foot, throwing the identity card on the road.

In the second position I am a protagonist making journeys into the unknown, searching for non-military solutions to a better future for those whose lives have been devastated by recent political events. Any traveller going on such journeys would immediately be struck by the tragedy and waste of attempting to force military solutions in countries where social and economic problems have become insurmountable. The numerous projects that I was attempting to start in these countries can therefore be seen as the efforts of a protagonist to find new solutions at smaller localized levels to benefit, as directly as possible, those who needed help to recover their normal lives. In every predicament the search for solutions was always guided by the simple proviso that the past as a reservoir of solutions is irrelevant. The challenge of survival could only be met if there is a constant search for solutions that are to be found not in history but in treasures that have to be brought down from the sky of the future. If the problems that seem to be erupting all around us are placed in and caused by history, then the solutions must surely be found outside that history.

The twentieth century seems to have finally concluded its span of years on rather hopeless prospects. It has been a century of boundless hopes as well as unprecedented violence and exploitation. In the west, it began amidst great optimism and ended with great pessimism. By the middle of the century, in the post-war period, the end of colonialism, followed by the undaunted rise of Pax Americana, was soon succeeded by the collapse of the Soviet Union and the continuous destruction of economies and communities of large parts of Africa, the Middle East and Asia. This was in contrast to the century's early years, when the energy of optimism was directly reflected in a number of activities, particularly in the creative arts, which were radically transformed by the shock of the avantgarde. As the century began, more accurately, between 1880 and 1914, the creative arts in Europe expressed a great sense of optimisim about the future. The nineteenth century had ended at a time when the faith in the machine age gave promise to believers in a great new future for mankind. The avantgarde was an indicator of the ever-renewing spirit of modernism. The machine age and its products were thought to be vital components in the coming utopia.

But the First World War ended that dream of a mechanized utopia. Millions of deaths were caused by the mechanical instruments of war machines. The mechanized utopia was soon replaced by a new utopia, a utopia inspired by the Soviet revolution and concerned more with social rather than with mechanical goals. The creative arts, particularly architecture, turned away from mechanically-inspired hopes and instead began to search amongst the images inspired by the high ambitions of socialism. The idea of a utopia has been important to modern architecture. Concern about communities needing to live in harmony in ideal surroundings amidst freedom from want and shelter had inspired much of the thinking about future cities in the early modern movement. The remarkable beginnings of modern architecture were grounded on the need for establishing a utopia. Utopian schemes were scattered across the drawing-boards of the pioneers of modern architecture. Some, including Le Corbusier and Tony Garnier, visualized entire utopian cities, while others, with Antonio Sant' Elia, Walter Gropius, Mies van der Rohe, Bruno Taut and Adolf Loos, designed futuristic buildings that became icons of modernism. In 1914, Sant' Elia wrote the *Futurist Manifesto of Architecture*, in which he defined the future house as something 'like an enormous machine'. In 1930, Le Corbusier submitted to the officials in Moscow a plan for a City for Three Million, which he called The Radiant City. Early Soviet pioneers believed that good architecture was important in solving the problems of social injustice.

Why then did the avantgarde, or even the whole of modernism, by the close of the century, come to be described as 'the late'? How did the revolutionary modern movement in the arts become enmeshed in corporate and institutional cultures? Had history really ended, as Fukoyama seemed to think? One answer could be that the pursuit of a utopia has always been a somewhat ephemeral ambition, since to live in despair remains unacceptable. The more recent tendency, to be indifferent to despair, is however a new phenomenon. It is not difficult to foresee that the growing indifference to suffering and the prevalence of voyeurism can be disastrous for architecture. Architectural concerns could get confined to the beauty of built forms alone. Such a narrow architectural concern could growingly emphasize only the brilliance and beauty of formal solutions. The designer's signature-building has already become a much-desired object for the corporate client. Following the leads given by *haute couture,* the architect's signature-building is already the primary concern for many luxurious magazines that publish new buildings.

Much of the material collected in the form of reports and diaries made during my missions remains unedited and is uninteresting for publication. Other more interesting material provided the gist for these essays. It was Rajen Prasad who suggested that I collect these essays in a book. During discussions with Rajen I chanced on Eric Hobsbawm's *The New Century*. On reading it, I was drawn to the clarity of his comments on the situation in the countries where I had spent the last four years. I am perhaps partial to his writings since he was once a teacher whose lectures I had attended. I liked particularly his opening remarks in the Introduction: 'It is part of life and business to question ourselves about where the future is leading. Where possible, we all make an attempt at it.' Further into the book, his reply to the Italian journalist Antonio Polito's question about the future of the state as an institution in the next century seemed pertinent:

> I believe that the disintegration of the states in these regions of the world is mainly the result of the collapse of the colonial empires, of the end of the era in which the great European powers controlled

large portions of the world, where they had found non-state governed societies, and had imposed a degree of external and internal order. This also applies to the territories conquered by Russia after 1800, such as the Caucasus. It is now clear that only in a few cases was this process anything more than an imposition from outside. In Albania, for example, there was no state before 1913 because there was no Albania. There can be no doubt that there was a functional state under the communist regime, even if it was perhaps the product of some compromise with non-state powers. But as soon as that regime disappeared de-facto, Albania was plunged back into a system of clan warfare, as occurred in Chechnya.

What has occurred in these parts of the world seems to be similar in some ways to what occurred in Western Europe following the fall of the Roman Empire. There was no longer any central authority. In some cases there were local authorities which still managed to function, and in other cases there was conquest by groups from outside which came to establish them. However, in reality vast regions of Europe lacked normal and permanent state structures for a long period of time. I believe that this is occurring again in parts of the world. This creates serious problems in relations with other parts of the globe where this is not occurring: Europe, America and Eastern Asia. It raises the question of interaction between the world where the state exists and the world where it does not. . . . It will therefore become increasingly difficult to know what to do in these areas, because effective intervention would require the permanent mobilization of forces which very few countries would be ready to maintain or would do so if their survival was at risk. For instance, Great Britain would never mobilize the same resources for an action in Kosovo that it used in Northern Ireland, because it is not as important. If you consider the cost of governing Bosnia after its war, with the cost of ruling a colony, you will realize that the difference is out of all proportion. I believe there were 64,000 foreign soldiers in tiny Bosnia, which was more or less the number required by the British to govern and maintain order in the Indian Sub-Continent.

The chapters in this book do not appear in the sequence in which they were written. The opening and closing chapters were presented at the ANY conferences in Ankara in 1998 and New York in 2000. The ANY conferences were a major event in the transatlantic debates on the contemporary situation of modern architecture. They began as annual events in 1991 and concluded in 2000. During these ten conferences, cross-disciplinary professionals met each year in a different city of the world to investigate the condition of contemporary architecture. The debates were published in a series of books named after the theme of each conference – *Anyone, Anywhere, Anyway, Anyplace, Anywise, Anybody, Anyhow, Anytime, Anymore* and *Anything*. The opening and closing chapters of this book have been published in two of the ANY books, and the opening arguments which appear in the first chapter, 'Abstract and Ancient Futures', are concluded in the last chapter, 'The Long Distant Future'. The four intermediate chapters describe in greater and more extended detail, the predicament of 'the modern' in different parts of the world. Beginning by contrasting the two projects of the Guggenheim Museum in Bilbao and the Iskcon Temple City in Mayapur, the text moves on to consider the persistence of the unmodern in Uzbekistan, Tibet, Nepal and India in the second chapter, 'Countermodernism'. The third chapter, 'Awarding Architecture', takes a broader view of the more recent international award recognitions that architectural projects have received. This was written after my participation as a jury member in the Aga Khan Award for Architecture in 1997. This award is quite distinct from a large number of international architectural awards. It is the largest prize offered for excellence in architecture in the world and has set a new precedent for giving recognition to non-formal architecture.

The last two chapters, 'The New Canaanites' and 'The Long Distant Future', illustrate the simultaneity of the two positions of the observer and protagonist that I refer to earlier in the text. 'The New Canaanites' contains observations and encounters of a specific conflict that I got to know well. It explores the futile efforts of two conflicting communities to invent their history and then to use that as a platform for launching a relentless military campaign to hammer that fictitious history into place as a solution for a future status. The protagonist in the text argues for the need to establish a united Canaan that is placed entirely outside the histories of both warring communities. The symbol of this New Canaan is expressed as an architectural project that benefits both communities and is located across the lines of conflict in Jerusalem.

Such a proposal inevitably raises the question of whether architecture can intervene in a political reality and thereby confront extra-architectural problems with physical solutions. The argument in the chapter proposes such an intervention as an answer. Since the deterioration in the relationship between the communities seems to occur incrementally, solutions too must be put into place such that their benefits are spread in an incremental manner. The proposed train and the proposed secular space of Jerusalem Station are conceived as the starting-points of such an incremental solution. The chapter explains the necessity of finding a hitherto unknown solution and it proposes taking the risk of exploring solutions that are other than dirty armed militia ones.

The abstract aspects of architectural solutions can sometimes be idealistic and futuristic. Architects are prone to dabble their skills in designing the unbuildable as concentrated, almost dense visions of their point of view. Such a venture into the unknown does carry its own risks. Perhaps the greatest risk is that of facing the ridicule of cynics that one inevitably encounters when one draws the future. India is merciless to its idealists and innovators. The smothering collective weight of a demoralized and cynical political and bureaucratic system squashes innovations. There is an almost unfathomable fear and distrust of a future that is disconnected from the past. Our enormous megalopolises have grown to inhuman proportions because visionary planning for a distant future is considered unnecessary. Thinking about the distant future is a lonely activity for any architect. Often it is a self-contained, almost private effort. But there are times when events are convened where these thoughts can be expressed and presented to fellow-professionals for their reaction. Two such events did occur, when I was able to formally draw up some of the ideas that would otherwise have remained within the privacy of sketchbooks. Both these occasions were conferences at which I chose to focus on Jerusalem and Kosovo: two places which are in the midst of intense military and political activities and are examples of collapsing countries reduced to chaos at the close of the twentieth century.

The architectural proposals for the Chabra house in Kosovo and the station at Jerusalem, which are illustrated in the last chapter, represent an effort to reach immeasurable goals in architecture. In a sense they represent those unattainable architectural goals that possibly hover on the edge of metaphysics. They respond to the deeper questions that architects ask themselves about the nature of the human condition and how to design and invent solutions to the human predicaments that spread themselves regularly across the front pages of our newspapers. There is perhaps need to explain the formal aspects of both designs. The reader may be somewhat confused by the appearance, in the last two chapters, of two entirely different forms for the same station at Jerusalem. Both solutions were developed together but elaborated one after the other. The initial form, shown at the conclusion of the chapter, 'The New Canaanites', was designed as a preliminary proposal and presented at the conference on Jerusalem held in Bellagio, Italy in 1989, organized by the well-known American planner Michael Sorkin. The second form was developed later for the New York ANY conference held in June 2000.

The city, as we understand it today, is a product of the nineteenth century and the subsequent industrialization process that transformed production relations in large parts of the world. Economics and architecture have always been intertwined in city planning. Change in cities is caused as much by ideas in urban and city design as by social inequalities, changes in transportation technologies and real-estate interests. Fundamental changes are required in the way we want to visualize our cities of the future and

these changes can only come about if there are radical ideas
expressed about the economy of cities and its links with new modes
of urban planning and production. It is therefore pertinent that an
eminent economist should write the first introduction to this book.
Prabhat Patnaik and I read economics at the same place, though not
at the same time. I have been a regular reader of his writings in
non-technical journals where he has frequently commented, with
great insight, on the contemporary world. It seemed natural
therefore for me to ask him to write the introduction to a book that
is about architecture.

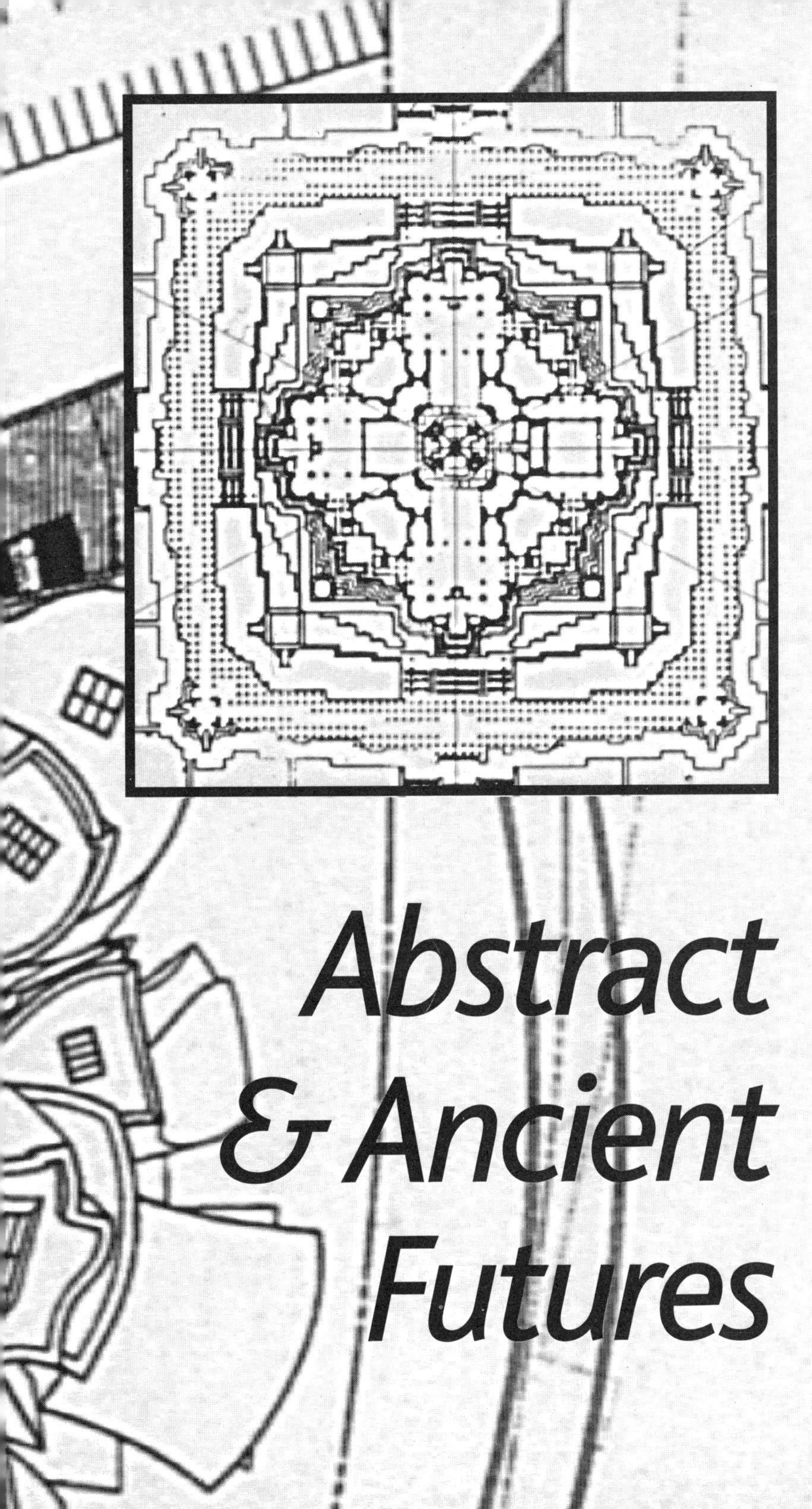

Abstract & Ancient Futures

Above:
'The history that lies silently in wait for us like a lion in the grass.' Image of a possible future by Bruce Pennington.
Below: Fragmentation of the World Trade Center on 11 September 2001: destroying the present for an undefined future.

Following what could be considered as the triple collapse of empire, socialism and time, a view of the world today shows that the advocates of modernism are being isolated as the 'ancients', or traditional societies, inherit the right to invent a future. This is a wide-angle, almost fish-eye view of contemporary activities in modern and ancient civilizations. It is necessarily historical and has to do with periodicity.

No matter what Bernard Tschumi says, history is not going to go away simply because late capitalism filled the void left by the collapse of the socialist project with globalization and simultaneity. Modernism does have a narrative, and its development and movement through time continue. The central character of the story cannot just step outside the story without losing his identity.

Globalization is increasing polarities. For example, the bipolarity of the Cold War has been transformed into the bipolarity of futures. It is possible to discern patterns of thought in this new polarity that are against plurality and view the relationship between contemporary time and future times as part of a bipolar view.

Futures are being projected, on the one hand, in the debates of the transatlantic nations and, on the other hand, in debates in much of the rest of the world. The transatlantic debates explore issues concerning the dynamism of the present, the potential for invention in an uncertain future and the accumulation of wealth. Meanwhile, large parts of orthodox Asia, Africa and the Islamic world have begun to reinvent ancient times, hoping for stability and constantly fighting the contemporary period's changing notion of measuring time. While advanced capitalist cultures explore the joys of choice and simultaneity in a new global environment, the less developed world is being asked by the voices of the orthodox to embrace their cherished spiritual assets and resurrect them for revelations of the future. As the Anglo–Saxon capitalist engine extracts surpluses from the lands and peoples of ancient civilizations, these countries defend themselves with cultural and religious assets supposedly contained in sacred books and practices. For these tired civilizations modernism is the claw of blasphemy and exploitation.

We have lived through the most violent and destructive century in human history. In it some 187 million deaths were brought about through human decisions and actions. The next century has started and the toll shows no signs of letting up. Of course, the twentieth century was also arguably the most exciting century. Entirely new systems of production and capitalism arose, were destroyed and rose again. A new socialist project, a pure philosophical invention, was conceived, born and has almost died. It was a century of enormous innovation, a period in which man's perception of time was reformulated. The First World War and the end of feudalism and ecclesiastical power helped to lay the ground for modernist beliefs. For modernism, mankind's future lies beyond the world of eternal stability and uninterrupted time. The passage of time and the natural environment are both within human control. Too many wars and revolutions had proved that divine stability and celestial time were unreliable guides for human destiny. It was in the twentieth century that the enormous destruction of life, property and human ideas enabled a new agenda to be adopted for the future. Since much of the destruction took place in Europe, it was natural that the new agenda – the modern agenda – should have risen from its ashes.

The theoretical, philosophical and empirical basis for defining the terms of the modern agenda had been laid before the Great War. The ideas for this foundation were contained in the disciplines of biology (Darwin), clinical anatomy, astronomy (Einstein), economics (Adam Smith, Malthus) and the avantgarde in the arts. The boundaries of knowledge about natural phenomena expanded enormously. The clinical dissection of the human body and the mapping of human organs opened up new potentials for intervening in the human body and its 'natural' life-span. In 1922, the first 100-inch telescope put an end to the idea that there were no distant galaxies. Not only were there no distant galaxies, there was also a large universe that, as Einstein argued in 1917, was expanding and in constant motion, a theory confirmed by Hubble in 1929. In all these new ideas the central issue was about dynamism and movement

Clockwise from top left: Adam Smith, Malthus, Einstein, Darwin

versus classical stability. Modernism proposed that the universe, the world and all human affairs are dynamic and hence capable of being influenced by human intervention.

In the non-Judaeo–Christian world, exactly the opposite notions began to take root. As colonial rule was withdrawn and as lands that had once been the territories of ancient civilizations (Arabic, Persian and Indian) regained independence, whole societies searched for their identities in ancient texts. (China, an exception, will not be discussed here.) As Judaeo–Christian societies began to redefine time as a brittle unit of measure, self-appointed prophets in much of the rest of the world began redefining perpetual, cosmic time.

As the European modern agenda developed further, it split into two streams. One was taken up by the imperialists who, through their trading offices, spread the new concept of clock-time throughout the Near, Middle and Far East. This stream is taking us into the twenty-first century. Modernism's other stream was the socialist project, which was intent on recasting society and creating a man-made future paradise. In order to realize that utopia, the present had to be destroyed.

The destruction of the present for the sake of the modernist future was inherent in both streams. The stream of the socialist project, of course, culminated in a dead end. This left the stream of the capitalist empire, powered by the entrepreneurs of western Europe and the United States, to lay a crust of modernity over the ruled territories, a superficial layer that began to peel off after the 1950s. Europe had paid a great price to modernize itself. The collective memories of at least two generations were gutted in the trenches, prisons and urban rubble of two world wars, one civil war and one revolution. Within three decades, two generations of young, educated and skilled minds were either wiped out or traumatized. The surviving children turned to the modern agenda to redefine their future.

The postwar period created new systems of education and new institutions, and introduced a hitherto isolated America into the affairs of the world as the most powerful modernizing influence. Coupled with advanced capitalism, America began to transform the globe. These changes had profound effects on the lands and peoples

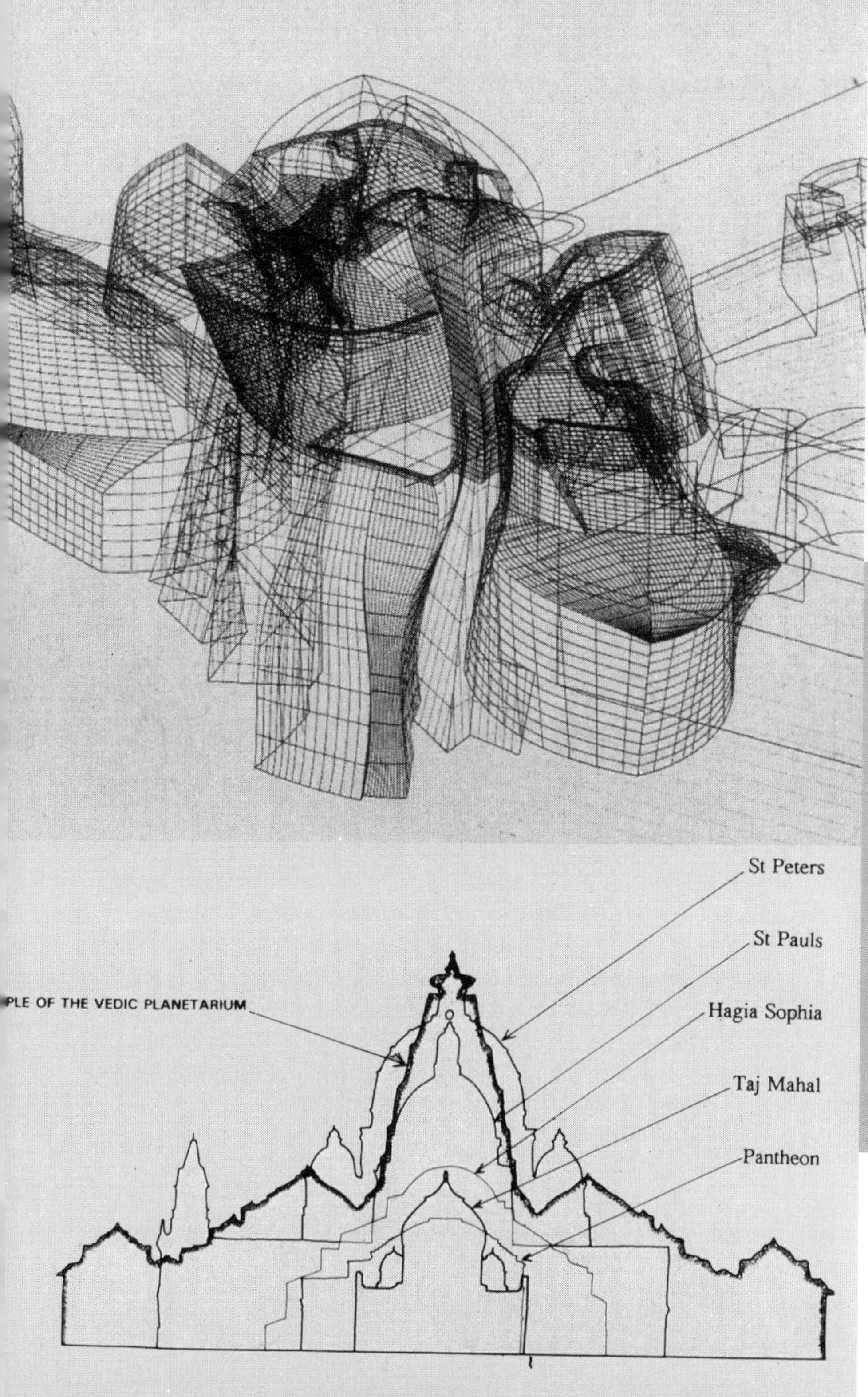

*Above:
Abstract computer-generated drawing of the Guggenheim Museum and the building as seen from across the river in Bilbao, Spain.
Below:
Outline profile drawing by Keith Critchlow of the Krishna Temple (dark line) shown in comparison with other world monuments.*

which had just been liberated from colonial rule. Imperialism's demise also ended the colonialists' sustained efforts to 'modernize' the colonies through the promised prosperity of private enterprise. The independent national leaders who emerged – Kwame Nkrumah of Ghana, Gamal Abdel Nasser of Egypt and Jawaharlal Nehru of India – faced a choice between two modernizing systems: the post-war American one and the Soviet one. Their choice was between the two currents into which modernism had originally divided itself. The original split in the modern movement defined one current with an ideological content that strove to redefine man to create a new paradise and harmonious equality; the other current improved technology to increase the accumulation of wealth, letting market forces sort out individual paradises. All three leaders chose the socialist project. Large parts of Africa and Asia saw in it the opportunity to define a new future – new in comparison to what their own theological systems of thought offered. It was also (with or without the political rhetoric), one way to adopt the modern agenda. Neither Africa, Asia nor the Middle East opted wholly for the corporate form of modernism. The modern agenda had only a materialistic content and no utopian ideology to counter the unmodern roots.

Today, the virtual collapse of the socialist project has exposed the depth of these unmodern roots and dried up one of the streams of modernism. In the non-Judaeo–Christian world, the institutions established by both colonial rulers and half-baked socialist rulers have begun to fall apart. As the crust of modernism flakes away, it reveals societies dominated by the unmodern that seem to want to cling to ancient wisdom to guide their destinies.

As we move toward the next millennium and as societies of the non-Judaeo–Christian world search for their identities, a faith in the divine determinants of time and futures is emerging. Ancient futures are being reformulated and reinterpreted according to traditional wisdoms, which are important sources of guarded information and control. These societies have not seen holocausts and the old social systems are, by and large, intact. Collective memory is relatively undisturbed. The deep roots of tradition and fundamentalism have

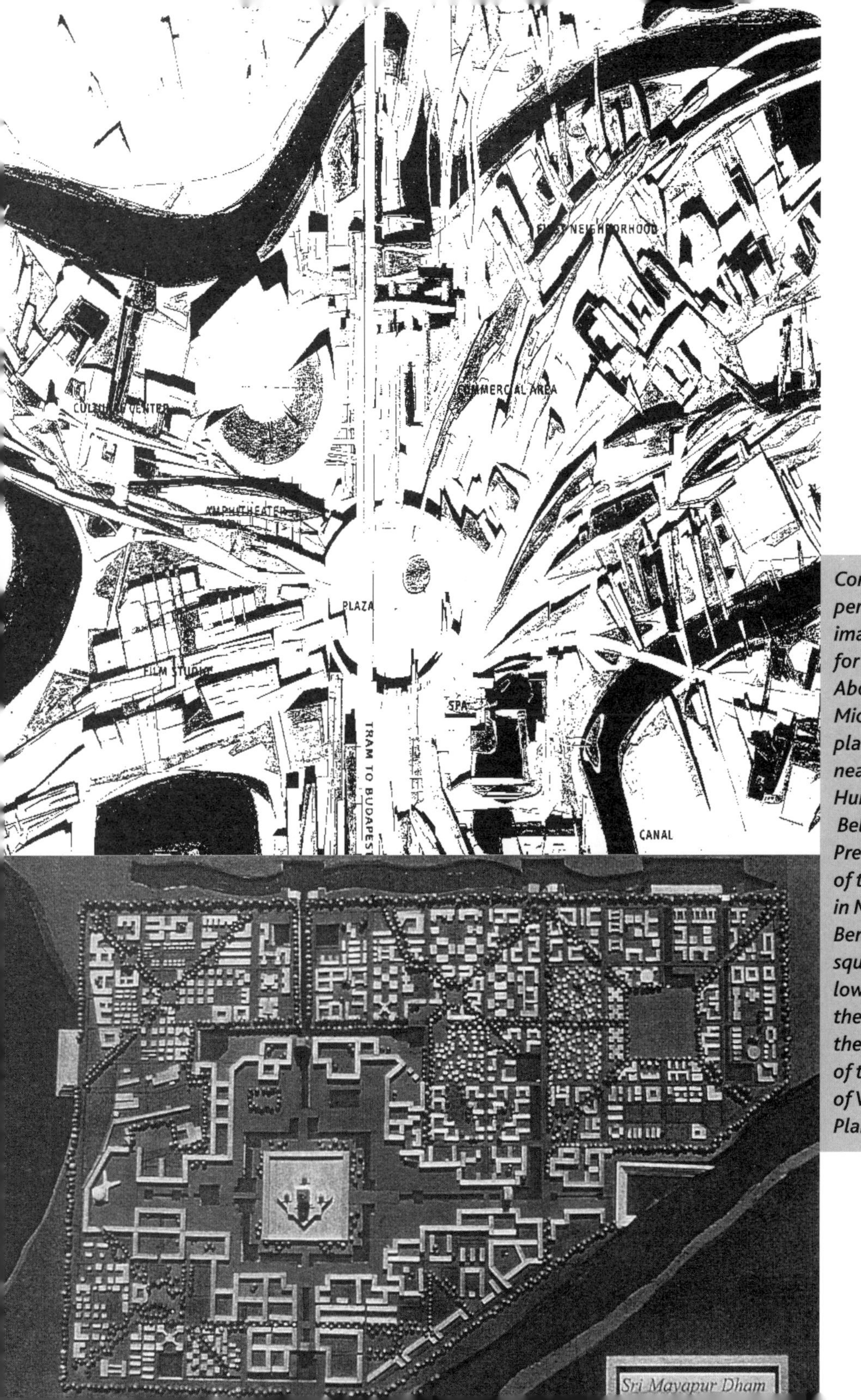

Contrasting perceptions and images of cities for the future. Above: Michael Sorkin's plan for Spa Tokay near Budapest, Hungary. Below: Preliminary layout of the Temple City in Mayapur, West Bengal. The large square in the lower centre of the city represents the footprint of the Temple of Vedic Planetarium.

begun to ensure that the modern agenda can no longer be adapted or grow easily.

Today, there are two basic versions of the perception of time and the projection of futures in global societies. The first, prevalent in western cultures, is formulated from the abstraction of the modern agenda and is disconnected from any divine suprasystem. The other, prevalent in large parts of the rest of the world (save, perhaps, China), is part of the ancient divine system resurrected in contemporary times. These societies are being encouraged to reject the modern agenda as a symbol of western exploitation and culture, and are increasingly advocating ancient futures. A duality persists between societies who believe in the modern agenda and those who shield themselves from the modern. It is possible to interpret this as part of a growing plurality, but I suspect more and more that this is going to be part of a narrative of irreconcilable differences.

The way futures are defined is closely linked to the way resources are invested: every investor places his bets on the future. Architectural projects are therefore quite unique because they symbolize the commitment of investors to a future resource. Two projects, the Guggenheim Museum in Bilbao, Spain and the Temple of the Vedic Planetarium in India, provide examples of the positions I have outlined here. Of the two projects, one is complete and the other is about to be built. Both are extremely important symbols of the future. One, the Guggenheim, is about abstract futures; the other, the temple, is about ancient futures. Both have been funded in unconventional ways. The one set in Europe is abstract in the extreme, its titanium forms generated by aircraft design software. It houses contemporary art from a museum system in New York and is set in the middle of Basque country, where an armed struggle is underway for regional independence from Spanish domination. The other, set among ancient temples, is a project of visions, built according to ancient geometric principles to last one thousand years. It is symmetrical, regular and promises salvation – an act of devotion placed in the cycle of cosmic time and immersed in local culture. It is a new city in which all the inhabitants devote themselves to worship and self-improvement.

Countermodernism
The Search for Authenticity in Central Asia, Tibet, India and Nepal

Above:
Guggenheim
Museum in Bilbao:
a shining knight of
abstraction.
Below:
Wooden model
of the Temple of
Vedic Planetarium
proposed for
Mayapur.

Wartime
destruction of
urban centres in
Europe provided
the ashes from
which the phoenix
of modern
architectural
abstraction
arose.

Conservation and contemporary architecture in Asia are increasingly becoming enmeshed in a common pursuit — to be 'authentic'. Since the whole of Asia would be difficult to cover in this essay, my focus here is on four regions: Uzbekistan, Tibet, India and Nepal. These regions are geographically contiguous but are today culturally and politically isolated from each other. Central Asia's Uzbekistan gained independence from the Soviet Union in 1991; Tibet was colonized by China in 1950; India has had more than five decades of independence; and Nepal was never really colonized. Yet, I hope to show that in all these regions conservation and contemporary architecture have become entwined, and the pristine principles of modernism are being obscured over by the rising dust of invented national identities arising from unmodern influences.

Conservation has become an important issue in Asia as nation-states compete for tourism revenues. The move to conserve buildings of the past had earlier been a concern of European scholars for many decades. A series of charters were drawn up to define the principles of freezing the architecture of the past. One of the more significant of these was the Venice Charter of 1964 which lists some articles in its text that seem difficult for an Asian conservationist to adopt

Facing page and above:
Postcard images of the wartime destruction of Frankfurt and the prewar condition of this area.
Below:
Postwar modern reconstruction of the same area showing reconstruction of selected buildings as reconstituted memorials to the prewar city and as concessions to the postwar conservationists.

without reservation. When twenty-two conservationists met in Venice more than thirty-five years ago, they formulated certain principles that they termed 'international'. Amongst these delegates, nineteen were Europeans, one Tunisian and two were from South America (Peru and Mexico). Asia, China, the Soviet Union, Germany and Great Britain were not represented. These meetings in Venice were prompted by concerns about the pace of postwar reconstruction in Europe, which was affecting not only the role of historic buildings but also the prospects for modern architecture. The sophisticated bombs that the Germans, British and Americans had dropped on each other during the war had devastated the historic urban fabric of European cities. Historical urban settlement patterns, which had taken centuries to evolve, were bombed to rubble. It provided the opportunity that modern town-planners and architects were awaiting. The American industrial complex had already embraced modern architecture unequivocally and Europe, the birthplace of the modern movement prior to the war, had to content itself with limited opportunities to demonstrate these ideas in built form. At any rate, many of the well-known and more articulate proponents of the modern ideology of architecture had already left for America before the war began. There they found the opportunity for the largescale projects and patrons they had looked for in vain in Europe (Ludwig Miës van der Rohe, Walter Gropius et al.).

The Venice conference was prompted by the concern of European conservationists to ward off the dangers both of uncontrolled modern redevelopment and reconstruction of postwar European cities in nationalist styles that would imitate the historic buildings that the bombs had removed. Modern architecture had to be given an opportunity, but it needed to be guided.

There was a felt need to draw a clear line between the past and the modern era in architecture. Modernist ideologies had always stressed the necessity of breaking with the past and of turning one's back on the decadence of decoration and symbolism that had 'infected' the architecture of premodern times. Abstraction, new building materials and functionalism were to provide the modern

Proposed Maitreya Temple project in Uttarakhand, India.

movement with new opportunities. Moreover, the movement also articulated its belief in *internationalism*. Regional influences that made the architecture of one country different from that of another were now to be a thing of the past – the future belonged to the postindustrial international movement.

Cultural reformations such as those that swept across Europe and transformed it into a region full of museums have somehow not blown across Asia in the same way. Living practices and the continuity of craft workmanship, whose roots go back many centuries, are still actively pursued on the strength of oral knowledge and written texts that have continuously been regenerated. Therefore it is inevitable that some of the sixteen clauses in the Venice Charter are difficult for Asians to comprehend or implement. The difficulties specifically arise from articles 9, 12, 13 and 15 in the section dealing with Restoration.

For various reasons, some of which I illustrate here, the shifting ground realities in many parts of Asia make it very impractical to follow the directives of these articles. Indeed, the sentiments that prompted the twenty-two scholars in Venice to adopt these articles are difficult for many Asians to support unless they are prepared to accept modernism unquestioningly. Consider the substance of these four articles:

> Article 9. '. . . The process of restoration . . . must stop at the point where conjecture begins . . . any extra work which is indispensable must be distinct from the architectural composition and must bear a contemporary stamp . . .'.
>
> Article 12. '. . . Replacement of missing parts . . . must be distinguishable from the original so that the restoration does not falsify the artistic or historic evidence.'
>
> Article 13. '. . . Additions cannot be allowed except in so far as they do not detract from the interesting parts of the building.'
>
> Article 15. '. . . All reconstruction work should however be ruled out a priori . . . only . . . re-assembling of existing but dismembered parts can be permitted. The material used for integration should always be recognizable . . .'.

Reteng Monastery in Tibet, famous for its association with Dromton, disciple of Atisa, who was known in India as Dipankara Srijnana, the greatest of the teacher-reformers of Tibetan Buddhism. This complex was destroyed during the Cultural Revolution of 1965. The photograph above was taken in the 1950s.

Jampaling Kum Bum Temple in Tibet before and after its destruction by dynamite. Obliteration of the roots and memories of the past was an important objective of the Cultural Revolution. This decade-long event permanently transformed the modernization process in both Tibet and China.

Master plan of Chandigarh by Le Corbusier monumentalized as a mural in the Chief Architect's office. The appointment of Le Corbusier was the first post-independence effort by India to capture a modern architectural future for India. More recently this effort is being abandoned in favour of invented pragmatic and pseudoclassical elements.

These articles direct the restorer to sharply distinguish, on the surface of the monument where he is intervening, the elements of the past from those of the present. Such a practice could be applicable in a Europe where the Renaissance, the Industrial Revolution and the fifty million deaths caused by two world wars have repeatedly wiped clean the slate on which living practices could have survived. But in most Asian countries such sudden catastrophes have not devastated craft beyond recovery.

This continuous link with the past may provide some explanation for the persistence of unmodernism which influences much of contemporary architecture in Asia. The techniques of building and the prevalence of craft in large parts of Asia are part of a persisting phenomenon. They are age-old, continuously developing, authentic, handcrafted and capable of endless adaptation to new styles. In these practices it is not easy to distinguish between conservation, preservation, restoration, reconstruction and contemporary formulations. The vast number of heritage monuments and buildings that are sprinkled all over southern Asia do not belong to some dead or forgotten civilization. In fact, many of them are often actively used by a contemporary society that coexists in a time and space that is simultaneously both modern and ancient. For instance, the sanctity of a site is considered more important than the kind of building placed on it. The continuous additions and alterations that are made to a structure which houses actively-worshipped deities are not perceived to destroy the sanctity of the site in any way. On the contrary, the stream of donations to a mosque or temple ensures that the structure is constantly altered and extended. Most actively-used ancient buildings of worship have evolved continuously over the centuries and will continue to do so. The presence of a worshipped deity makes the need for a growing pilgrim infrastructure around the image subservient to the importance of the divine presence.

The conservation principles that got formalized in the Venice Charter cannot possibly be applied to all ancient structures in Asia.

Nevertheless, during the colonial period institutions were established to propagate the European view about preserving the past. The Archaeological Survey of India is one such institution which sought to take on the responsibility of preserving the past according to the principles set down by modern Europeans even before charters were written. In other countries that extended across Central Asia, the Soviets and the Chinese established similar institutional frameworks. However, there was one significant difference – both the Soviet and Chinese governments set about an active campaign to destroy the past. It is ironical that the intensity of the effort with which a society desires to create museums of the past is somehow matched by an equal intensity to destroy remnants of the past. The deliberate and thorough destruction of many of the remains of the past that occurred during the Industrial Revolution, the two world wars and the communist revolutions in Russia and China, simultaneously created some of the most remarkable museums in existence. In China, during the decade of the Cultural Revolution (1965–75), over 3,000 Tibetan monasteries and temples were dismantled and destroyed. Soon afterwards a massive programme was commenced to convert the Potala Palace (left relatively unharmed) into a museum. Similarly, in the Soviet Union the destruction of church buildings was matched by converting the Kremlin into a monument to the glory of the achievement of the workers under the czars.

The belief in modernism was forged by the rapid process of obliterating a past which had become discredited. A unified and coherent set of beliefs was formed with an unshakeable trust in an idealized future that the industrialization of nations would make possible. In many countries in Asia, this unshakeable trust was adopted by the newly-emergent political leaders who intensely desired a European future for Asia. Kemal Attaturk had already paved the way, it seemed to them, in Turkey. Jawaharlal Nehru, in India, set about blueprinting the future. He invited Albert Mayer and then Le Corbusier to lay out a city for the future of India. It was a decision made from the conviction that the past needed to be left behind and that the future lay in the urban utopia of Chandigarh. Pakistan asked

Samarkand.
Above:
Before the Soviet takeover: a silk route market town that traded with India and Central Asia.
Middle:
Soviet rule brought modern theories of town planning to Central Asia. The urban fabric of the past was torn down and only selected historical buildings were identified to be preserved as museums of a 'premodern' civilization.
Below:
Bokhara, like Samarkand, had its historical housing quarters cleared to set off the preserved museum monuments in an open plaza.

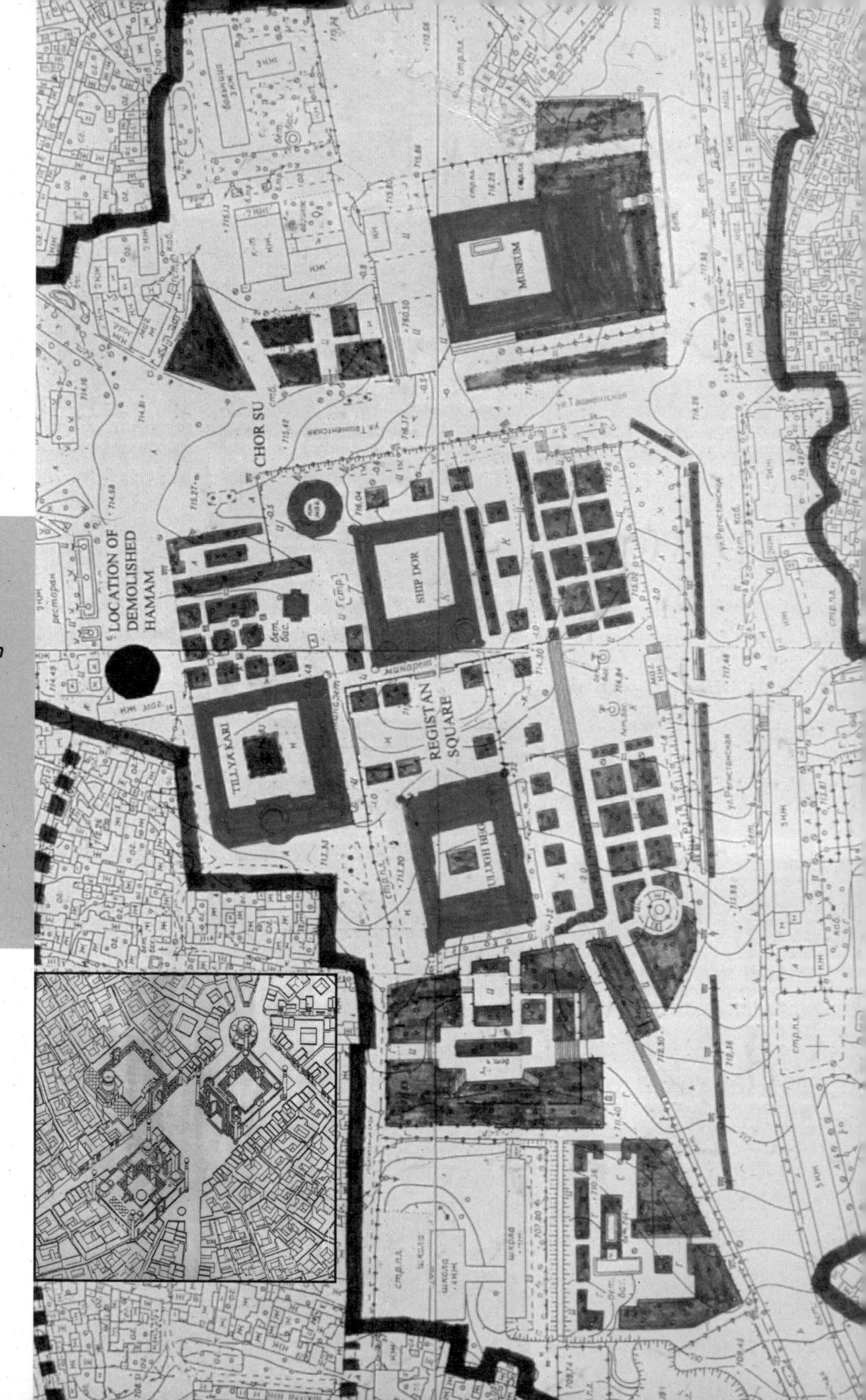

Soviet Samarkand-period demolitions of mohallas (within thick black line). The Registan monument is conserved as a museum. Inset: Drawing of presumed mohalla prior to demolition.

*Reinvention of the Uzbek national identity.
Above:
A new shopping arcade built in brick with traditional pointed arches. Bricks have become a national symbol of a lost identity and their revived use in buildings seeks to reinvent the glory of Timur.
Below:
A modern Soviet-designed building is resurfaced on the outside with bricks and arches to reflect the newfound Uzbek identity.*

Above:
Bibi Khanum Mosque in Samarkand. This Timurid mud-brick building, which collapsed soon after Timur's death, is being reconstituted with concrete arches.
Below:
The podium of Lenin's statue survives, capped with a nondescript cupola after the statue was knocked down. Timur has replaced Lenin as the national hero of Uzbekistan and Kazakhistan.

Constantinos Doxiadis to plan Islamabad and Louis Kahn to design the legislature building in Dacca.

However, in all these countries, the heroic efforts to try and capture a modern European future which had no links with the past seem to have lost their moorings. The past could not be destroyed; unmodernism persists.

In the precolonial period, Central Asia, Tibet and India were part of a region that was collectively influenced by the civilizations of Arabia, Persia, India and China. These were the regions through which the strands of the silk route brought cultural influences. However, by the middle of the nineteenth century, gunpowder and the lure of lucrative trade brought in the colonizers and isolated these civilizations from each other. Henceforth these regions became, for a century and a half, recipients of modern cultural beliefs and practices that had originated in Europe. Through the two communist revolutions modernism became an ideology, and postindependent Indian leaders too began to believe that European ideas could take root in the east. However, as the twentieth century came to a close, in the period following the collapse of the Soviet Union, this unshakeable faith in a modern socialist world seems to have been discarded. As the backlash of religious fanatics makes its presence felt, a renewed and strengthened belief in unmodernism has begun to be important.

In a curious way, conservation and contemporary architecture have been allied in the search for cultural roots. Modernist ideologies seem to be suspended in architecture. In suspending these ideologies, many architects have accepted that their creative efforts ought to spring from the architectural heritage of the past. Ironically, these architects were all educated in the modernist idiom in schools of architecture whose syllabi had emulated Bauhaus teachings. Despite the fact that Bauhaus teachings regarded the past as something fit only for museums, architects in Asia schooled in this belief have begun to link their contemporary work to premodern forms and ideas. Much of contemporary Asian architecture remains agonistic and its authors desperately seek attention. The relative absence of

Inventing authenticity at the Potala in Tibet. The Potala is the most powerful cultural symbol of Tibet. The ancient images of Srongstan Gampo (above) and his Nepalese queen (below) have been reauthenticated. Both images to the left show the new Sino–Tibetan features and dress of the first Buddhist rulers of Tibet. The images to the right were taken in 1952 before the recent drive to reauthenticate Tibetan history.

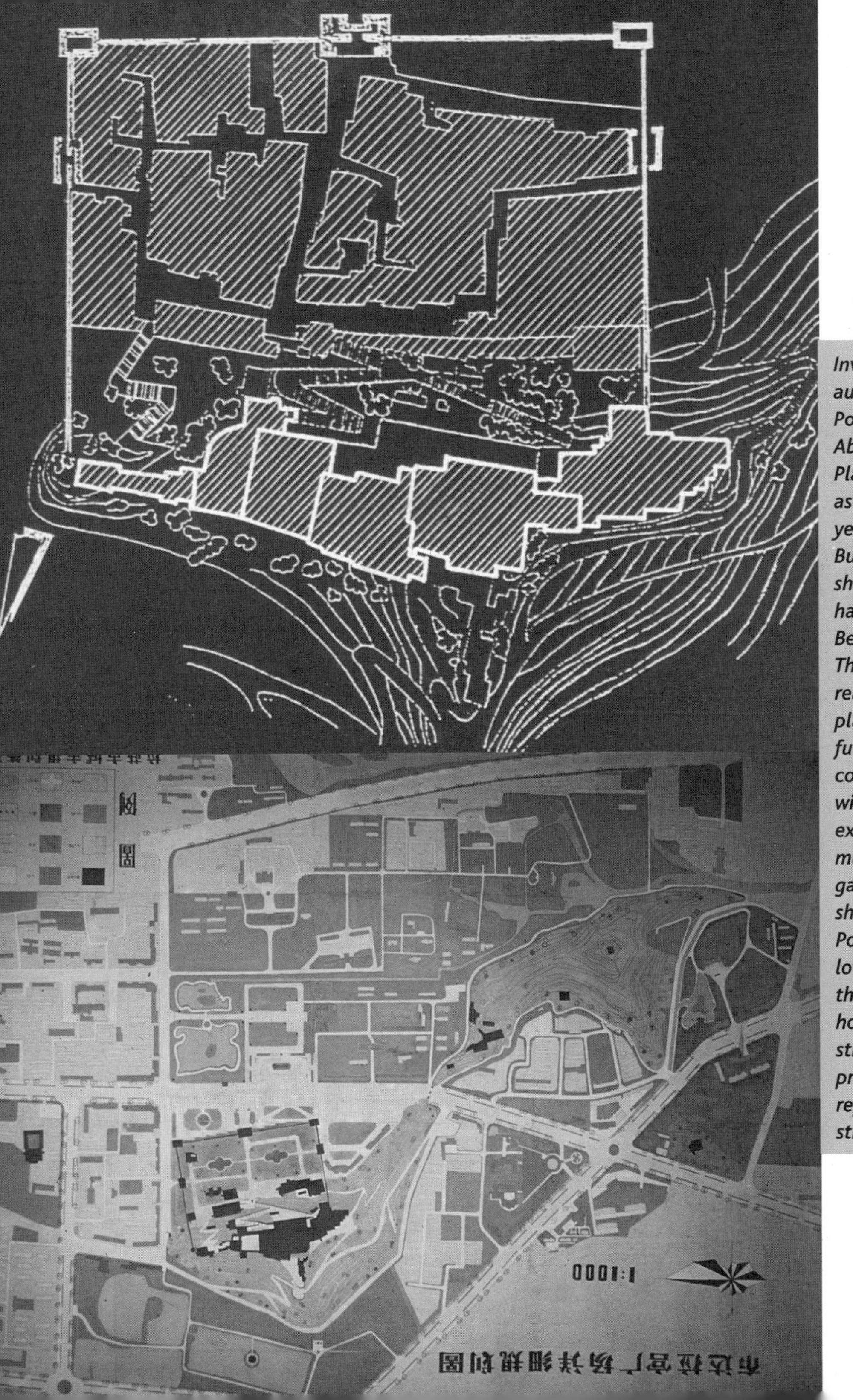

Inventing authenticity at the Potala in Tibet.
Above:
Plan of the Potala as it existed some years ago. Buildings are shown in diagonal hatched lines.
Below:
The proposed reauthenticating plans for the future Potala complex set within an extensive municipal-style garden. The dark shaded building of Potala in the lower centre of the plan shows how the irregular streets of Shol are proposed to be replaced with straight streets.

Inventing authenticity at the Potala in Tibet.
Above:
The eighteenth-century mural image of the Potala within the palace complex has been arbitrarily chosen as the model for reconstituting the Shol village area at the base of the Potala.
Below:
Ongoing process of reauthenticating: Shol buildings being constructed out of concrete block and clad with regional-style facades.

The persistence of the countermodern in the recent temple constructions: the Mata Temple in Delhi (above) and the Sri Adya Katyayani Shakti Peeth temple at Chattarpur, Delhi (below). The style and features of these buildings are components of the paraphernalia of ancient futurologists.

architectural critics and magazines has encouraged architects to express and elaborate on explanations of their work. Growingly, these explanations describe sources of inspiration that are unmodern.

Another way to describe this persistent faith in countermodernism is to term it the invention of authenticism. Authenticism in one's work seems to relieve the agonistic nature of contemporary work. 'Authentic' here can also be described as 'entitled to acceptance' and 'of unsuspected value'. While the Soviet Union was in existence, invented authenticity was confined to the restoration and reconstruction of monuments, and modern buildings were built to replace the old urban infrastructure. But after 1991, the authenticating practices seem to have spread from the confines of the monuments to influence contemporary architectural work. Formulating independent national identity has set off searches for roots and expressions of national identities.

Under Soviet rule the restoration effort in Central Asia, (Uzbekistan, more specifically), was concerned with inventing authenticism. While entire parts of historical cities were bulldozed to make way for modern buildings, certain museum areas were identified in Bokhara, Samarkand, Khiva and Kokhand and reconstructed as open museums about the past. The practice of reconstructing these monuments contradicts every rule in the Venice Charter. Remnants of the past were stripped and replaced with new imitative parts. Ancient Timurid bricks were intermixed with contemporary bricks. Ceramic tiles were remade and used to cover areas where there were no traces of tiling. The Bibi Khanum Mosque in Samarkand built by Timur in 1398 had portions of it changed within two decades of its construction. In the nineteenth century, when the czarist forces invaded Samarkand, it was blasted by cannon-fire. Today, the whole structure is being rebuilt with concrete reinforcement in the minarets and arches, as an authentic symbol of Uzbek architecture.

While Uzbekistan had been a Soviet colony the invention of authenticism was confined, more or less, to monuments which were selected by the administration to be museums of the past. Extensive

Facing page: Contemporary architects invent authenticity for their buildings by explaining dubious connections between their work and historical monuments. Above: Legislative building of the Bhopal Assembly, designed by Charles Correa. Below: CIET building in Delhi, designed by Raj Rewal.

Reconstruction of
historic monuments
as modern artefacts.
Facing page, above:
Detail of internal
structure of the Mandap
pavilion in Durbar Square,
Bhaktapur, Nepal.
Above :
Reconstructed Mandap
pavilion. Gotz Hagmuller has
designed a new historic
monument using modern
materials and techniques.
Facing page, below:
Hagmuller's steel columns
in the reconstruction of
Patan Museum in Nepal.
The original wooden
column is placed
alongside to emphasize the
contemporary intervention.
Below:
Elevation drawn prior
to reconstruction of Patan
Museum.

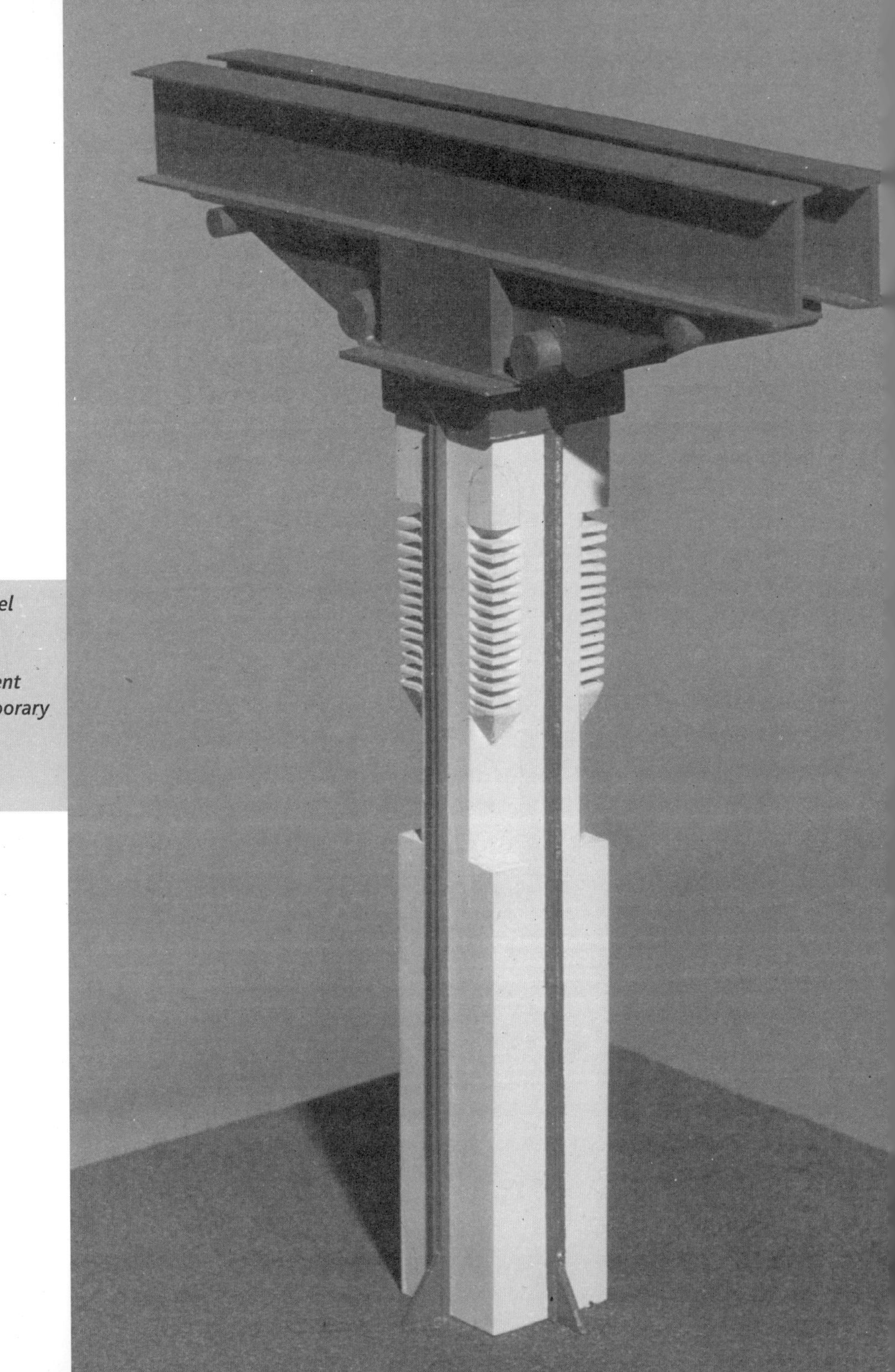

Model of steel
column with
timber
embellishment
in a contemporary
hotel in
Kathmandu,
Nepal.

brick-manufacturing facilities dedicated their production to supply materials for reconstructing the monuments. Bricks, ceramics and wood-carving resources were developed to feed the restoration–reconstruction process. Contemporary architecture, on the other hand, was built primarily out of precast concrete in a continuing effort to modernize the Uzbeks. However, under this modern surface, the attachment to unmodern architecture persisted. Even before 1991, when Uzbekistan unwittingly woke to independence, these bricks, originally meant exclusively for reconstruction, had begun to find their way into contemporary buildings such as the Hamza Theatre in Kokhand, designed by Sergo Sutyagin. By 1991, this effort to invent authenticism had become a secure part of contemporary architecture. The buildings which have been put up in the last four years have begun to clad their facades in brick to resemble past monuments as part of the new Uzbek identity. Modern buildings built in Soviet times have been reclad in brick and pointed arches have been added to authenticate them in a newfound Uzbek style. The reaction against Soviet rule and modernism has resulted in the reinvention of a new Uzbek style of architecture with imagined links with the past, with clues taken from the museum monuments which had earlier been reconstructed by the Soviets. Traditionally, Uzbek buildings were made in mud and timber, while brick was used primarily as a cladding material for monuments such as mosques, *madrassas* and *khanqas* (monasteries). A return to a real authenticism was clearly out of the question, as mud could hardly be identified as the authentic building material for an independent Uzbekistan. So brick, readily available from kilns which had once served the Soviet restoration effort for the museum monuments, became the new authentic building material.

East of Uzbekistan lies the Tibetan plateau, a region that has had long historic links with ancient Sogdiana, now Uzbekistan. Czarist forces had occupied this territory which they considered as a vulnerable underbelly – Central Asia – in the mid-nineteenth century. They did not attempt to occupy Tibet since the British forces, led by Francis Younghusband (who occupied Lhasa in 1904), had issued a clear warning to Russia to keep its hands off territories close to India. After the British left India in 1947, the Chinese colonized Tibet, in 1950. Chinese rule brought modernism to this isolated region. The decade-long Cultural Revolution destroyed almost all the historic monasteries and temples in Tibet. Like the Soviets, the Chinese too identified building complexes which were then emptied and maintained as museums. The Potala and Sera monasteries in Lhasa are probably the best known of these examples. As in Uzbekistan, enormous resources were spent on authenticating these buildings with new colours and construction techniques that were modern and that violated the principles of the Venice Charter.

Perhaps the most interesting example of a structure that was transformed from a traditional Buddhist temple to a simple modern one and then again to an ancient one, is provided by Samye, one of the most sacred temples in Tibet. Samye, first founded in the mid-eighth century by Indian gurus, was originally a pagoda of three levels with temples one above the other, decorated in Indian, Chinese and Tibetan styles. The structure was capped with a timber pagoda roof. During the Cultural Revolution, Samye was transformed into a simple block and stripped of all its decorative embellishments. The pagoda roof was dismantled, perhaps in an effort to sever its links with an Indian past. It was left with a flat roof and a band of red on the parapet, much like an ordinary Tibetan building. Then, in 1980, the unmodern past reasserted itself and the entire pagoda roof was reconstructed. At the same time temples and monasteries began to be reconstructed in the style of buildings that had once existed there. Since the monasteries that were destroyed during the Cultural Revolution decade were not recorded accurately, Tibetan nationalism began to assert its presence by rejecting the modernist buildings of Lhasa in favour of a style that could be termed an invented authentic Tibetan style.

Unlike Uzbekistan and Tibet, India has had more than five decades of freedom and democracy. It is a vibrant and open country ready to accept the most diverse influences because it has not been subjected to coercive rule since 1947. And yet, even in India, a nation with its own satellites in space and nuclear power, unmodernism continues to extend its influence over contemporary architecture. The enormous increase in building activity at places of worship confirms the suspension of modernism. The architectural form of these new temples evokes non-existing prototypes conjured up in a pastiche of architectural elements. They evoke authenticity by inventing forms that have their origin somewhere in the past. These historical forms are easily manipulated, reassembled and stamped with the authenticity of an iconography that looks historical, except that it is constructed entirely out of cement, plaster and concrete.

Even contemporary architects have felt the need to explain their works of architecture by using justifications linking them to history and thereby inventing authenticism. The construction of temples and mosques in styles that evoke authenticity is perhaps understandable because they are intended for worship, surely an ancient activity. However, in contemporary architecture, where modern functions are required to be accommodated, buildings are being conceived, built and justified as structures that have invented connections to the past. Charles Correa explains his new Nehru Museum in Jaipur in the language of the *Vastu Purusha Mandala* (derived from vedic science), and his IUCCA building in Pune in terms of cosmology. Raj Rewal's CIET building in New Delhi is inspired by the 'haveli' architecture of Jaisalmer, while Uppal Ghosh has designed the Anandgram complex in Delhi as a traditional rural environment complete with thatch and mud walls. Unmodern authenticity and modern abstraction seem to be placed on opposite sides. While relying on the building technologies and materials that modernism propagates, Asian architects seem to embellish these materials with unmodern authenticity. Rewal's CIET building is perhaps a good example: the reinforced concrete framework has sandstone cladding whose references to an unmodern Rajasthani architectural vocabulary are unmistakeable. Such a position may seem contradictory or confusing because it spans both modernism and unmodernism, but it would seem less so perhaps if it is viewed as an unmodern stance. This is amply clarified by two European architects who have been working in Nepal for the last decade and a half. Niels Gutschow, a German, and Gotz Hagmuller, an Austrian, decided to demonstrate, in the purest form possible, their belief that historic evidence can be reinvented with modern and unmodern materials used together. Both architects, taught in the modern ideology of Adolf Loos's architecture, came to a Nepal which seeped into their work, and they began 'to enjoy adornment and take pleasure in ornamentation', to work on an architectural vocabulary that could be defined as eclectic historicism, with a defined syntax that is both unmodern and modern.

The eight-cornered Mandap pavilion which stands at one end of the Durbar Square in Bhaktapur was constructed between 1988 and 1990. It replaces an earlier version that was completely destroyed in an earthquake in 1934. The design and construction of the new pavilion was made possible because there were sufficient photographs and drawings available pre-dating the collapse, which enabled the architects to create a design that was authentic and yet invented. The new structure is supported on a steel frame built to withstand seismic forces, on the basis of sophisticated analysis and designs made by Walthar Mona at Darmstadt. Thus, a historic building was reinvented with the aid of technologies and design analysis that are modern. The self-confidence reposed by the designers and builders in a modern technical solution was based on a belief that unmodern adornment has an important function to play in our lives. The Mandap is clearly a building of the industrial age because its entire steel structure is exposed to view from within. The building is 'a mixture of a steel-girdered structure with a façade made from individually prefabricated parts formed by hand from wood and terracotta'.

Having designed and built the Mandap, Gotz Hagmuller went on to tackle a much larger project – the museum building at Patan, where one wing had been so badly damaged that it needed reconstruction. However, instead of attempting a historical reconstruction of the type done by Soviet restorers in Uzbekistan, Hagmuller boldly strode into the project questioning the very basis of historical reconstruction in a manner that hid modern interventions. He designed the replacement of the collapsed wing as a contemporary act of architecture, using concrete and steel. But not in the aesthetic of modernism: he unified the aesthetic of the past and the present, creating steel columns in the form of the traditional timber ones. Modern technology was clearly expressed. But it was not used to propagate the abstraction of modernism. Instead, the material was used to demonstrate how the aesthetic of a Patan historical building could comfortably ride into the twenty-first century using new materials and without being fossilized in the past. Hagmuller was not being authentic, nor was he inventing authenticity, nor was he being unmodern. He was simply demonstrating what the word contemporary can mean for architecture in Asia.

Awarding Architecture

here is a prevalent view that the Aga Khan Award for Architecture is concerned with promoting a third debate in architecture. This debate, articulated for instance so clearly by Charles Jencks in 1996, argues that the award is 'the third way – the veritable multilaned highway' which is pluralistic and hence identifies architectural projects that span a wide range of typologies. By giving approbation to the Modern Institut du Monde Arabe in Paris as well as the adobe Great Mosque at Niono, the award is seen to encompass 'multilaned' contemporary architectural activities that could be relevant to the developing Islamic world. Since the award recognizes conservation projects, social housing and innovative contemporary architecture, as well as other types of work, it does seem to have become the symbol of a broad, pluralistic architectural patronage. The award's third position is defined in the context of the transatlantic debate about modernism at one end, and the regional debates on authenticity, cultural continuity and craftsmanship at the other. This so-called third position is supposed to occupy the middle ground between these two debates, and also to promote debate and an exchange of ideas that try to reconcile the two seemingly irreconcilable positions. Dubbing the award 'middle ground', 'third way' and 'pluralistic', is therefore easy to understand. Over the last seven cycles, the award has recognized more than 70 projects in different parts of the world. With every jury report which explains the reasons for choosing the projects, the message of the award is broadened and diversified. The societies that form the constituency of the award are themselves very diverse; thus the award takes care to publish its juries' deliberations and reasons in the form of debates on issues that can bring together diverse concerns for diverse societies.

The third way is one way of seeing the Aga Khan Award as part of the newly-emerging, seemingly pluralistic direction in architecture that includes modernism, regionalism, housing, conservation of historical buildings, urban planning and landscaping. This image of the award is a 'comfortable' or easily acceptable one that would please and make sense to the largest number of people.

Above:
Institut du Monde
Arabe in Paris,
France.
Below:
Niono Mosque.

Since it is culturally and stylistically non-specific and represents more a basket of ideas than the sharp edge of a specific viewpoint about architecture in a global context, the award's position in the global debate can be interpreted as one that shifts.

The global debate is an important reference point because it presumes not only global participants but also participants who are engaged in a debate about core issues relevant to architects. The global debate is generated by engines of private capital which are geographically located in the west. They provide the essential ingredients of the debate, which are patronage, media coverage and engagement in critical discourse. The media constitute a global network; thus, architectural events such as the inauguration of the Guggenheim Museum at Bilbao, Spain, become global events.

This dynamic partnership between the media and architecture is a recent phenomenon. The media have their own requirements, and for architecture to be important it must be iconic, a clearly identified product, the centrepiece of debate and, of course, politically significant.

The nature of the debate about contemporary architecture has changed significantly in the last two decades. During the fifty years after the Russian Revolution, the central debate that concerned post-Bauhaus architecture was primarily about the ideology of modernism and its international significance. Until the early 1970s, even though postwar capitalism had restructured itself and Europe had significantly recovered from the damage of the Second World War, the ideological content of modernism was concerned with avantgarde positions and proposals based on socialist ideas of reformulating societies. Municipal housing proposals, leisure activities and urban-scale projects were concerned with reformulating futures, which had always been an important concern of socialism. However, the socialist project could not recover from its internal contradictions. The process of collapse began with Soviet tanks entering Budapest and it gained momentum until *perestroika* and *glasnost* finally dismantled it completely. As the process of discrediting the socialist project

Above:
Current urban
developments in
Jakarta,
Indonesia.
Below:
Tony Garnier's
industrial city.

Children of Kosovo
learning private
enterprise.

gained strength, it became increasingly difficult to defend egalitarian futures as architectural ideals. While capitalism restructured itself and put an end to its internal rivalries – which had precipitated the war – and as the epoch of Pax Americana began to gain momentum, the social concerns of architects were dispersed in diverse directions. The New Left emerged as a symbol of resistance to the increasingly privatized west and tried to bundle together the dispersed pluralistic issues about regional identities, the environment and resistance movements that had broken away from the communist ideology in the 1960s. Successive conservative governments then began to tear down social security nets and infrastructure and to let them out to the private sector. The state was replaced by the private sector as the more significant patron, and the architectural profession lost its most important client. In the decades following the implementation of privatization all over Europe, corporate clients emerged as champions of modern architecture and architects had little option but to narrow their concerns and jettison the inconvenient ideological stance that promoted ideal egalitarian futures. In a sense, the architectural debate became detached from the central debates about culture, social and economic issues and futures in western societies. Having lost contact with the New Left, modern architecture began to be deeply enmeshed in corporate architecture and crafting with new building materials.

The new corporate clients of architecture stripped modern architecture of its social concerns but hailed and encouraged its great formal qualities and its potential 'designer signature status'. International finance capital, faced with underlying unemployment and accompanied by sluggish growth-rates in almost all the advanced countries, turned to the untapped market of millions of potential Asian consumers. International financial institutions rode out for opportunities in Asia and launched massive architectural projects in Southeast Asia and southern China, which are nearing completion. Modern architecture, now on a back-burner in the social debate, became an inseparable partner in the economic development of Bangkok, Shanghai, Canton and a host of other coastal centres in Asia where capital arrived from the west in search of higher returns. The buildings that responded to the growing needs of the finance sector became major icons in the banking world. They exhibited a wide range of stylistic hues, but they also belonged securely to modernity.

These are the mega-projects of today. At one time, Tony Garnier and Le Corbusier had visualized the mega-projects of modernism as ideal cities of industrial workers. The Asiatic and particularly the coastal urban developments of Canton and Shanghai see these contemporary mega-projects as the new territorial conquests of international finance. They are international in their funding, design, construction and staffing, but their achievements do not seem to form any part of the global critique of architecture. Nowhere are the architectural programmes of these mega-projects linked to concern about the common people whom socialism championed.

It remains apparent that enormous poverty is still prevalent in the Asiatic world as well as in the Islamic world. Concern about their present condition and future cannot simply disappear or become a question of charity just because the socialist project has disappeared. Perhaps the Aga Khan Award represents the only, and rather lonely, articulated position that holds that architects still have broader responsibilities in developing societies. It is just possible that the award is *not* trying to carve a 'third way' that spans from modernism to tradition. Instead, it is possible that the award's importance lies in clearly articulating an alternative debate about the relevance of architecture today. It seems apparent that the award is questioning the narrowing of the debate in modern architecture and is instead initiating a dialogue about a contemporary architecture that is more relevant to the problems of development. This would naturally influence the choice of geographical areas where such a debate could be relevant. By confining its search to the boundaries of the Islamic world, the award is virtually signalling its own constituency as being at

least one contemporary part of the world where the broader
social issues of architecture can be practised and discussed.

These broad concerns are going to become crucial to the
global condition in this new millennium. It is possible to argue that
the social concerns reflected by the award-winning projects are
globally relevant. African economies have collapsed because their
food security system was devastated. The entire former socialist
bloc is experiencing downward-spiralling economies that have
reached a precarious situation, with unemployment as high as 30
per cent in places where 'structural adjustments' are being
hammered into place. Millions of precast multistoreyed housing
blocks, jerry-built in the 1960s and 1970s, are beginning to crack
and flake. This enormous region, on the border of Europe, has had
its national income reduced to a third of its former size; its
enormous social infrastructure, built over the years, has all but
collapsed; poverty is rampant; and mafia gangs control the
economy. In the present millennium, these are the places where
societies have to be given new futures. These new futures cannot
and will not emerge out of the patronage of international finance
capital. It is possible, however, that these futures can be articulated
by the broader concerns of architecture that give importance to
community involvement: craft, rebuilding of old urban centres,
social housing and self-help. The award could be considered as a
keeper of the conscience of architecture, documenting in its
debates and published materials the relevance of architecture in
developing societies.

In its announcements of winners over the last seven cycles,
the Aga Khan Award has identified a wide range of projects, with
each jury shifting its emphasis in different directions. However,
common to all these directions is concern about the past, present
and future. By including conservation, social projects and innovative
contemporary buildings within its terms of reference, the award has
defined a broader perspective of architecture that is important to
formulate now that the transatlantic architectural debates are
strongly influenced by the interests of global finance and media

projection. The award uses an elaborate system of identifying projects for its consideration. Nominations followed by technical reviews and a series of jury meetings for each cycle ensure that a project is not viewed simply as an abstract model of form. Context, function, social relevance and regional importance are all considered criteria for excellence. By a process of inclusion rather than exclusion, the award has been able to identify a reforestation project in Turkey as well as a lepers' hospital in India which used minimum resources to create a structure for the benefit of the outcasts of society.

Despite the clear intentions of the award to formulate its own message in the world of architecture, the impact of its significance in the global debate remains somewhat difficult to identify. Successive juries have been concerned with trying to measure the contribution of the award's message to the international architectural discourse; the sixth and seventh-cycle juries were concerned with 'universal relevance and contribution to the architectural and the social discourse of the world'. The distinction between the architectural and the social discourse is important. In the realm of the architecture of buildings, models of the western world continue to dominate the major issues of architecture in the developing world. Buildings designed by western or, in some cases, Japanese architects continue to be iconic models for most architects in the rest of the world. On occasion, when the Islamic world offers its territory for the creation of world-class architecture, an architect from the west has been commissioned to build for the benefit of Islamic or secular societies within the context of the Islamic world. In 1998 the jury clearly took a position that world-class buildings responding to the problems of change in the Islamic world had yet to emerge. In considering architectural projects, therefore, the jury clearly intended to imply that the importance of the buildings, of which there were five, was regional. In other words, the jury was not attempting to place buildings of excellence in a regional context into a global context. It was not searching for pluralistic or 'third way' messages to tie together regional

Rehabilitation of Hebron Old Town, a symbol of restored Palestinian roots under siege by Israel. Jews claim the right to control access to the tomb of Abraham within the mosque (below).

Tuwaiq Palace in Saudi Arabia, one of the recipients of the Aga Khan Award for Architecture in 1996.

Projects
recognized for
their excellence
by the Aga
Khan Award:
Slum Network
programme in
Indore, Madhya
Pradesh, India.

Above:
Lepers' Hospital
at Chopda Taluka,
Madhya Pradesh,
India.
 Below:
Legislative
Building, Bhopal,
Madhya Pradesh.

Above:
Khuda-ki-Basti,
Karachi, Pakistan.
Below:
Grameen Bank
beneficiary in
Bangladesh.

architectural activities. On the contrary, the citation of these five buildings implies that their significance is confined to their regional context, a context within which their excellence should be judged. The jury had split its search into two categories. One category had importance within the territories that form the constituency of the award; the other with 'recognizing projects that had a wider global context and meaning'.

The two projects, 'seen to have qualities that could be of relevance to a broader global context', were essentially concerned with the reclamation of community space. These were projects of state patronage removed from the world of international finance and essentially concerned with social issues. They have global significance because they are concerned with issues related to the reformulation of communities within the increasingly archaic nation-state.

In awarding these two projects for their broader universal values, the jury acknowledged the need for architecture to address questions of community-based egalitarian futures. By recognizing the community as the accelerator of change in architecture, the award is drawing attention to a contemporary architectural activity that the transatlantic architectural debates have long forgotten. Therefore, the message is not a pluralistic third way. It is a dualistic message which implies that the universal concerns of architecture are its social concerns, which must be clearly distinguished from regional architectural aspirations.

Both the projects – the Rehabilitation of Hebron Old Town and the Slum Networking of Indore City – transcended their local contexts to generate solutions that have important symbolic values. Where, for instance, a designer or institutional catalyst substantially involves a local community and transforms with its help a deteriorating slum environment into a beautiful space, the practice of architecture also becomes a social or ideological act. More importantly, such work begins to redefine a significant symbolic role for architects as critical players in the reconstruction of community futures. When one considers the enormous damage done to the urban communities of Europe in former Yugoslavia or northern Ireland, or considers the growing demands for the recognition of community identities such as that of the Basques, one also realizes that there is no way to revitalize these communities without the intense involvement of professional people who act as accelerators in the process of bringing together communities in conflict. It is difficult to visualize other significant ways in which the growing homeless and jobless populations can be given hope in both the developed and underdeveloped parts of the world. Projects with a predominantly social content and in which degraded environments are transformed for the benefit of the poor and the outcasts are crucial architectural achievements. The heroic role of architects and voluntary agencies in improving environments through a collaborative design process needs acclamation and serves as a reminder of the broader role that architecture has to play in the development processes of all societies.

In rewarding such projects as Khuda-ki-Basti in Karachi in 1995 and the Hebron and Indore projects in 1998, the Aga Khan Award continues to emphasize that the universal message is a symbolic one that relates to bringing communities together. Because community conflicts are increasing rather than decreasing in all parts of the globe, the symbolic significance of social projects transcends regional and national contexts. The model of the Grameen Bank Housing Programme, awarded in the fourth cycle, is more important as a global model than as an individual building confined to a regional context and commended for its architectural merit. The universal message of the award is therefore contained in the recognition of these social projects. These can be regarded as symbols of hope in a world in which the structures and boundaries of nation-states are being reformulated. Newly-aware communities with narrower cultural identities are struggling for recognition that is separate from the identity of the nation-state that once included them in a larger national identity. These community identities could become the building-blocks of regions in this millennium.

Museums for Another Future

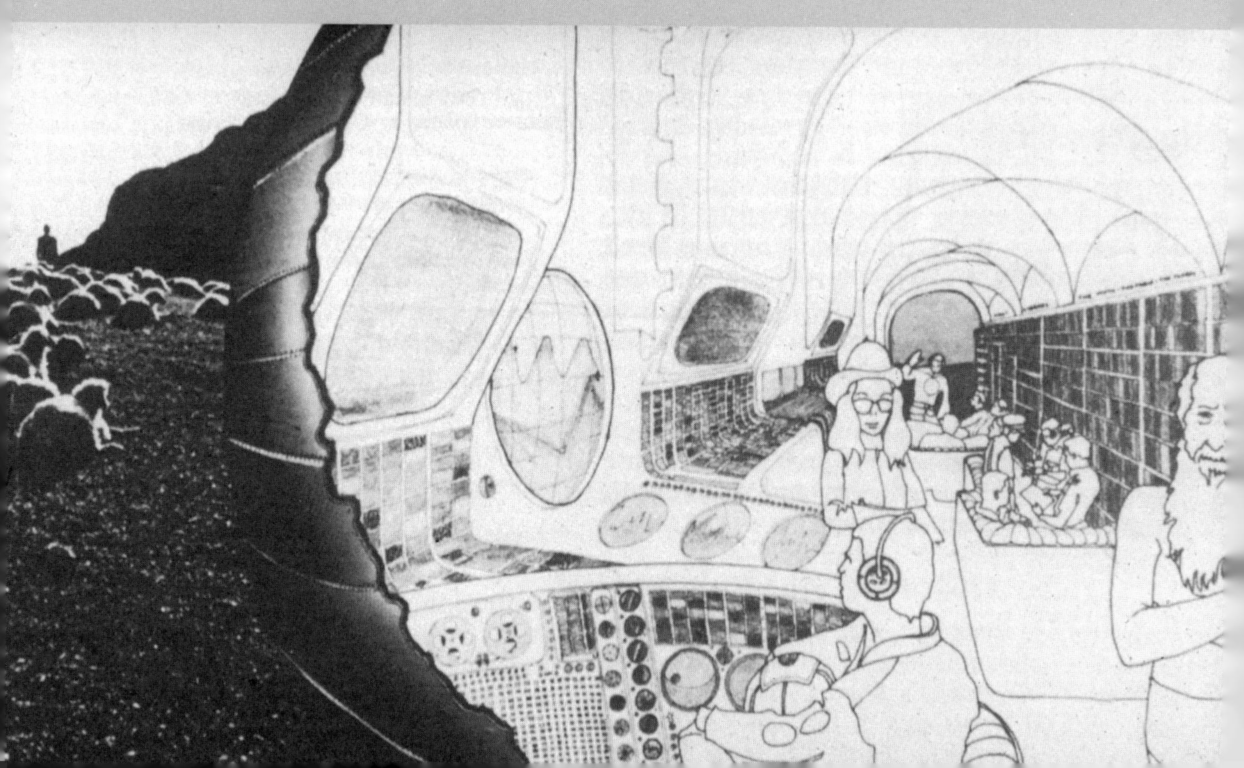

This is an essay about transformations from the present to the future. More specifically, about possible transformations of our inherited institutions. To begin with, let us consider some questions that could be in the minds of many of us. The first question that has been nagging me, ever since I first discussed museums with Neville Tuli, is one that will obviously have occurred to many of us – 'Why are our museums so utterly irrelevant to our present times?' And then, following that – 'How can we transform all this social investment into something relevant to our future?' And then perhaps a final question, and this one interests me the most – 'What sort of new museum concepts should we be thinking about if these institutions are to be relevant once more?'

I am making a distinction between two separate problems. One concerns the resurrection of our existing dinosaur museums and the other is about how to create completely new kinds of museums for our future.

This essay is arranged in four parts. The first part looks at the founding of the present museum and its fossilized state that reflects outmoded nineteenth-century European thinking about knowledge of art history, culture and science. The second part looks at the vested interests of the nation-state in leaving these fossils undisturbed. Third, I move on to that favourite double-edged sword which has only recently begun drawing blood in this part of the world – globalization, and how it is impacting on museums. The last part of the essay is purely speculative and opens up ideas for the future.

Somewhere around the end of the nineteenth century in Europe, a new professional concerned with the study of human social behaviour – the sociologist – began to appear as a self-standing academic who did not wish to stand under the umbrella of any of the classical disciplines. It was roughly the time when economics too was emerging as a separate discipline. The study of human social behaviour began to be accepted as a 'science'. It was introduced into European discussions and writings, at the initial stages of acceptance, as a 'cultural science' which included the new disciplines of sociology, anthropology and psychology. It was termed a cultural science to distinguish it from 'natural science' which deals with chemistry, physics and biology. The natural sciences deal with the study of nature and the cultural sciences seek to study human-made objects. By terming these cultural inquiries a 'science', the new academic aspirants wanted to elbow themselves into a position that was on a par with the science of nature. The natural sciences believe in studying nature objectively through mathematics, empirical experiments and instruments of magnification such as the telescope and the microscope. Cultural scientists too began to base their methodology on so-called objective and empirical data. For instance, native heads were measured and compared to the measurement of exhumed skulls of cave-dwellers. Races were arranged in linear sequences of cultural development, their objects were categorized and, most important of all, a theoretical framework was formulated to structure all of culture. We are all familiar with the racist findings of Darwin, the sexual obsessions of Freud and the arbitrary social formulations of Max Weber. Thus emerged the cultural museum – a collected resource of cultural man-made objects gathered in the field from expeditions and journeys in the colonies. The museum was a resource which enabled a more leisurely pace of research to be carried out in an environment that was safe from the flying mosquitos, spears and arrows of the bush and the forest. The British Museum is perhaps the best and greatest example of such an institution.

During the years when Europe colonized Africa and Asia, imperial adventurers set forth into the tropics and brought home to their metropolises not only vast anecdotal material written in travel diaries but also extensive collections of bought, stolen and plundered objects. The diaries, of course, went to established libraries. All the new material however needed to be placed within a new type of container where the oriental and African collections could be collated and catalogued. So the cultural museum became a storehouse of material which could be accessed by this new discipline of scientists. A theoretical framework could then be explored that would place all this new information within a worldview that scientifically confirmed the superiority of the European race and its culture.

The cultural museum therefore became a safe treasure-house for a vast volume of movable objects which had been plucked out of their original context. These were then stored as fodder for the slowly-grazing social scientists whose capacity to digest all this stuff was naturally limited by their ability to chew and extract the theoretical juices.

The emergent art gallery was not in the same situation. It had risen from the earlier eighteenth and nineteenth-century salons in the private homes of the aristocracy, from private collections of paintings and sculptures which had been gathered for the personal enjoyment and social status of the owner. But the beheading and emasculation of the European aristocracy robbed the artist of his patrons. The state had to intervene and the national art gallery emerged as a museum of portable sculptures and easel-paintings which were owned by the state or by private foundations. Later, private foundations could benefit from art investments without attracting excessive taxation. The Louvre, the National Gallery and the Prado are perhaps the best examples of early art museums of the state. The Prado Museum in Madrid, for instance, opened as a private art gallery of the royal family in 1819 and it was not till 1868, when Queen Isabella was driven into exile, that it became the property of the nation.

These early painting and sculpture museums of course contained only European art. Later, the bounty from the colonies began to overflow from the rooms of the private mansions of imperial explorers and administrators, and the collections eventually passed on to a new kind of oriental museum. Perhaps the Victoria and Albert Museum in London is a good example, just as the Musée Guimet in Paris is, of this type of museum of non-European art.

Both cultural and art museums as we know them today are barely 150 years old and, in their present form, represent the greatly expanded institutions of nineteenth-century Europe. They were transplanted into India as typical European state institutions and we in India are fortunate that they exist at all, even if in a fossilized condition. I say this because my speculations about the future of museums are not influenced by the colonial origins of our museology. It is not a question of colonial versus national. It is quite clear to me that we have built our nation-state on the foundations of institutions that were grafted here as transplants only in the last 100 years. We have gained immeasurably from the experience of these grafts. We have probably lost a lot too, but the effects of those losses are hard to gauge.

Consider our museums of today as transplants, but nevertheless parts of our national body-system. The question is, what sort of organs are they and how vital are they to us?

To the question 'what sort of organs', I would reply – today they are symbolical representations of outmoded nineteenth-century ideas of looking at a society through randomly selected portable objects. These portable objects are cultural specimens preserved in jar-like showcases so that a few people can enjoy them and others can use them for research or for conducting through groups of giggling children. To the question 'are they vital to us?', I would reply yes, because they can provide us with the root-structure to regraft new institutions for the next century or two. They do represent the accumulated social capital of this country and on this great things can be built.

Today we display museum objects as preserved specimens. They have been removed from their context, quite often damaged or fragmented, and yet they are supposed to illuminate a history. They are dated, physically described, numbered and placed under surveillance. By viewing them we are supposed to become cultured. Effectively, what is being said to the viewer is: 'Here is a randomly selected object that has been retrieved from our past. Look at its beauty, what a great past we had.'

Future museums need to explore a completely different relationship between the object and the viewer. This new relationship could question the assumption that a sense of eternity is present in the object on display, which has actually been plucked out of its

Assembly Hall (tsug-lha-khang) at Tabo Monastery in Spiti, Himachal Pradesh. The hall is a three-dimensional version of the Dharmadhatu mandala. Stucco images on the wall are elements of the universe of the mandala.

*Image of
Aksobhya from
the Royal
Academy
catalogue of the
exhibition,
Retrospective
of the Sacred
Art of Tibet: Art
and Compassion,
held in London
in 1992.*

context and placed within a 'jar'. The future museum could, rather, enhance the deep sense of eternity that lies within the inner mind of the viewer. In a sense, the objective of a presentday museum to try and give knowledge to the viewer through the historical and descriptive framework needs to be reviewed. My contention is that the real sense of deeper knowledge that can be given to the viewer by simulating the context is equally important as bombarding him with historical information that tries to describe the context.

Let me illustrate this with an example. A seated figure of the Buddha as Aksobhya was shown at the Retrospective of the Sacred Art of Tibet held at the Royal Academy in London some years ago. (I shall discuss other aspects of this exhibition later.) The figure is an eleventh-century painted wooden carving from either Ladakh or Spiti. It is an object plucked out from a three-dimensional *mandala*. The main prayer room, the *tsug-lha-khang,* at Tabo in Spiti, is such a *mandala* showing the deities of the *Dharmadhatu mandala*. This is the context of the solitary portable figure on view.

The exhibition/catalogue description says: 'Seated Buddha. Western Tibet. Third quarter of eleventh century. Height 21.5 inches. The Cleveland Museum of Art. Andrew and Martha Holden Jennings Fund.' A further description informs us that 'The Buddha is tensely alert, seated in the diamond posture. His right hand is placed over his knee in the earthwitness gesture.' And so the description goes on . . . 'The figure appears animated and vigorous, but his visage is introspective and calm' . . . etc.

Now, a completely different description of the same object could read thus:

> In the ethics of Buddhism, man is constituted of six elements – earth, water, fire, wind, space and understanding (*vijnana*). This figure of the Buddha is one of the *Dharmadhatu mandala* deities of Vairocana's palace whose internal space was contemplated upon along with all forces present in the circle of deities. This contemplation brought fulfilment and omniscient knowledge. The initiated, being familiar with the six elements, could then perform rites and be initiated in the *mandala*. While contemplating this *mandala,* the disciple conjures up

in the eastern doorway the Buddha of the blazing golden sun colour
and the thirty-two characteristics, wearing an orange robe, teaching
while seated on a white lotus sea . . . etc.

It is my contention that the second description begins to work
towards a change of emphasis from the eternity in the object
towards a deeper meaning and context that is closer to our own
understanding.

Emphasizing our great lost national heritage and our destroyed
glorious past as the central concern of our museums is hopelessly
misplaced. Museums need to be about the eternal values of
knowledge and creativity and the relationship of our modern world
to these values. Museums should not be about the propaganda of
nationalism. Such propaganda objectives are the concerns of
governments that want to counter modernism, change and creativity.

This brings me to the second issue: the vested interest of the
nation-state in preserving these museums as specimen-racks of our
golden past. Museums as institutions of the modern nation-state are
a recent phenomenon. The degree of control that a government
exercises on them is a direct function of its desire to exert its
centralism and authority. The more power and control a government
exercises over museums, the more it wants to counter new ideas
about culture, and the more it seeks to portray its own version of
culture. Today, the Archaeological Survey of India, the National
Gallery of Modern Art and the National Museum are headed by
professional bureaucrats who, as we well know, are the repositories of
the universal conscience of India. However, to illustrate the absurd
lengths that a nation can go to, to invent its great past, I would like
to illustrate an example from Israel. I use this example with care
because similar issues are being raised in our country and to me it is
quite feasible that this could be the shape of things to come.

The best example of a nation-state museum in which a state is
sponsoring a cultural agenda is the museum housed in the Tower of
David in Jerusalem. Here the state of Israel has projected a historical
narrative about Jerusalem that is tied together with objects and
images placed in a script that was written before the objects had

Invention and formation of identity through imagined and cooked-up history.
Above: Tower of David Museum in Jerusalem which exhibits images of the tenth-century BC imagined City of David.
Below: The Third Temple, which is to be rebuilt at the site of the Haram Sharif.

been found. Israel was formed in contemporary times by gathering together flocks of communities which had been grazing in different pastures of the globe for hundreds of years. Their colour, language and culture have nothing much in common; it is therefore necessary to invent a common history and place it within the walls of a museum to authenticate it. The modern state of Israel needs the imagined history of a single undisputed narrative to overcome the deep differences among themselves because they come from more than 80 countries and are white, black and yellow in colour. The museum has the clear intention to lay claim on Jerusalem and that claim is based on rather dubious historical inventions.

On the evidence of some excavated rough stone walls in a tiny area, a claim is made by the museum, based only on the biblical texts, that the City of David stood at a particular site.

On the evidence of the traces of a foundation and enormous walls made in Roman times, a claim is made that it was the site of the great Herodian Temple.

However archaeologists say, and I quote: 'The opulent empire founded by David and developed by Solomon seems to have left no trace whatsoever in the archaeological record . . . the material culture of the initial phase of the Israelite Iron Age . . . is remarkable for its extreme impoverishment and lack of aesthetic sensibility.'

Despite this observation, the image of the Second Herodian Temple is represented as a massive palatial structure with a sophistication of detail that is not impoverished at all.

As a sequence to the narrative about the main Jerusalem Temple, there is another museum dedicated to the destroyed Second Temple and the coming Third Temple. The images here project the imagined Third Temple that is to be built at the site of the Haram Sharif, the third most sacred spot for all Muslims.

The official state-run museum abounds in projections of speculative history. Here I have taken just two examples to illustrate how a nation can use a museum to block debate, discussion and research, to propose an invented past and to use this invention to oppose cultural change. Such a state will not let go of central control of its key museums.

Fortunately, however, there are changes going on in the outside world that do not regard national agendas as being of overriding concern. I come now to the issue of global change.

Photography, colour reproduction, internet, movements of global finance, privatization, the collapse of socialism – all these and more have transformed the national dreams of every country and made them subservient to external impacting. Obviously, any museum unaware of these changes and unable to relate to them must perforce remain a dinosaur. However sceptical one is about globalization, one cannot ignore that in our country this phenomenon has paralysed the possibilities of alternate radical national strategies. The judgement that the international community may pass on our national programmes has, more or less, restricted our independence in economic matters. The question is whether cultural issues too will get equally paralysed. I wonder whether soft-pedalling on the ridiculous project of the Ayodhya Temple is influenced by the possible adverse judgements that international investors and donors might pass.

Globalization will, it seems to me, determine three issues that will affect the museum of the future: issues of territory, communication of centrally-propagated ideas and the impact of media electronics and speed.

Perhaps the best illustration of the issue of territory is the Guggenheim Museum in Bilbao. This is a museum designed by Frank Ghery, an American architect, paid for by the Government of Spain and located in Basque country, which is in the midst of an armed struggle to assert its regional identity, in the town of Bilbao, surrounded by the decaying structures of abandoned factories. The collection of objects belongs to the Guggenheim Foundation of New York and they manage it. The issue of territory has two consider-ations – first, the physical use of state territory which, as we can see in this case, is only notionally national, and second, the right of the museum to own what did not originate in that territory but was brought there. For instance, to whom do the Elgin Marbles belong?

The most important issue that is going to face us Indians, so proud of our national heritage, is whether the objects in our museums will soon be regarded as part of a global heritage by those who are interested in extending rules about heritage protection into a global territory. Are we not going to see national culture being superseded by a global culture? I do not mean this in the sense of a homogenized global culture. Rather, in the sense that pro-globalites will see the diversity of culture as an essential component of a global culture within which national rights need to be subjugated. Thus the responsibility for the care of cultural objects and sites assumes international ramifications. Perhaps I exaggerate!

Democracy has become a desirable global objective and that is enough of a criterion to justify destroying a nation that does not have it. Basmati and neem are now parts of the private global empire. Is it possible that the framing of a global agenda for cultural ownership is not too far behind? Because, if the rule-makers do not quickly formulate this agenda, then they will have to return so much of the stolen and plundered material that is sitting in their museums – the Elgin Marbles, the Amaravati carvings, the Pharonic images, and so much else.

We, as a nation, will have to resolve these issues amongst ourselves at a high level fairly soon. Otherwise the thinking in this entire area will be determined by the Hindutva stormtroopers who will scream in agitation about how our glorious culture is getting defiled by McDonalds and Deepa Mehta's films.

Leaving aside the issue of territory, I turn now to the issue of centrally-formulated ideas. For some years now, museums in the west have begun to change and to introduce the concept of the 'commercial viability' of all new museum-based events. The impact of the market economy and the unification of communications around the world have begun to provide us with events of a new order. There is an increasing shift towards a polarization of the increasingly centralized or institutionalized propagation of cultural ideas on the one hand and, on the other hand, a growing atomization of the multidisciplinary creators and artists or individual owners of heritage objects. The mega-retrospective is perhaps the best example of this trend, and I shall illustrate this with just one example in a field that I am engaged in.

An important international exhibition, Wisdom and Compassion: The Sacred Art of Tibet, was organized by the Royal Academy of Arts, London, the Asian Art Museum of San Francisco and Tibet House, New York, in association with Harry N. Abrams Inc. Publishers, New York. This was the most comprehensive exhibition of Tibetan art ever seen in the west and produced a landmark volume as its catalogue. It contained groundbreaking scholarship on one of the world's most interesting civilizations. The exhibition presented 160 portable objects from museums around the world and private collections. The 400-page lavish publication will of course long outlive the exhibition itself. The catalogue as a critique is more important than the objects, which are only momentarily assembled from many countries and then dispersed in heavily-insured crates. No collection is therefore complete and the idea of the civilization or context can only be put across if such a mega-event takes place. But let me explain a little more the subject of Tibet.

Tibet, for nineteenth and twentieth-century Christians, represented the closest proximity to the lost paradise, Shangri-La. Imagined in the European mind as a land of purity and mysticism, its remoteness and inaccessibility added to its image as the elusive paradise. Of course, the Chinese occupation in 1959 put an end to all that. But because the Dalai Lama escaped, the idea of this civilization continued to exist in the western mind. The exhibition is a representation of this civilization that indeed exists only in the minds of the promoters and the exiled. The promoters called it a 'modern civilization', just to introduce its relevance in the contemporary world. The fact is that this civilization has been forcefully dispersed by the Chinese. However, commercial interests of the west in China today inhibit placing the context of this collection of objects in the real world of the destroyed land.

Isn't it time that we in India began thinking about new

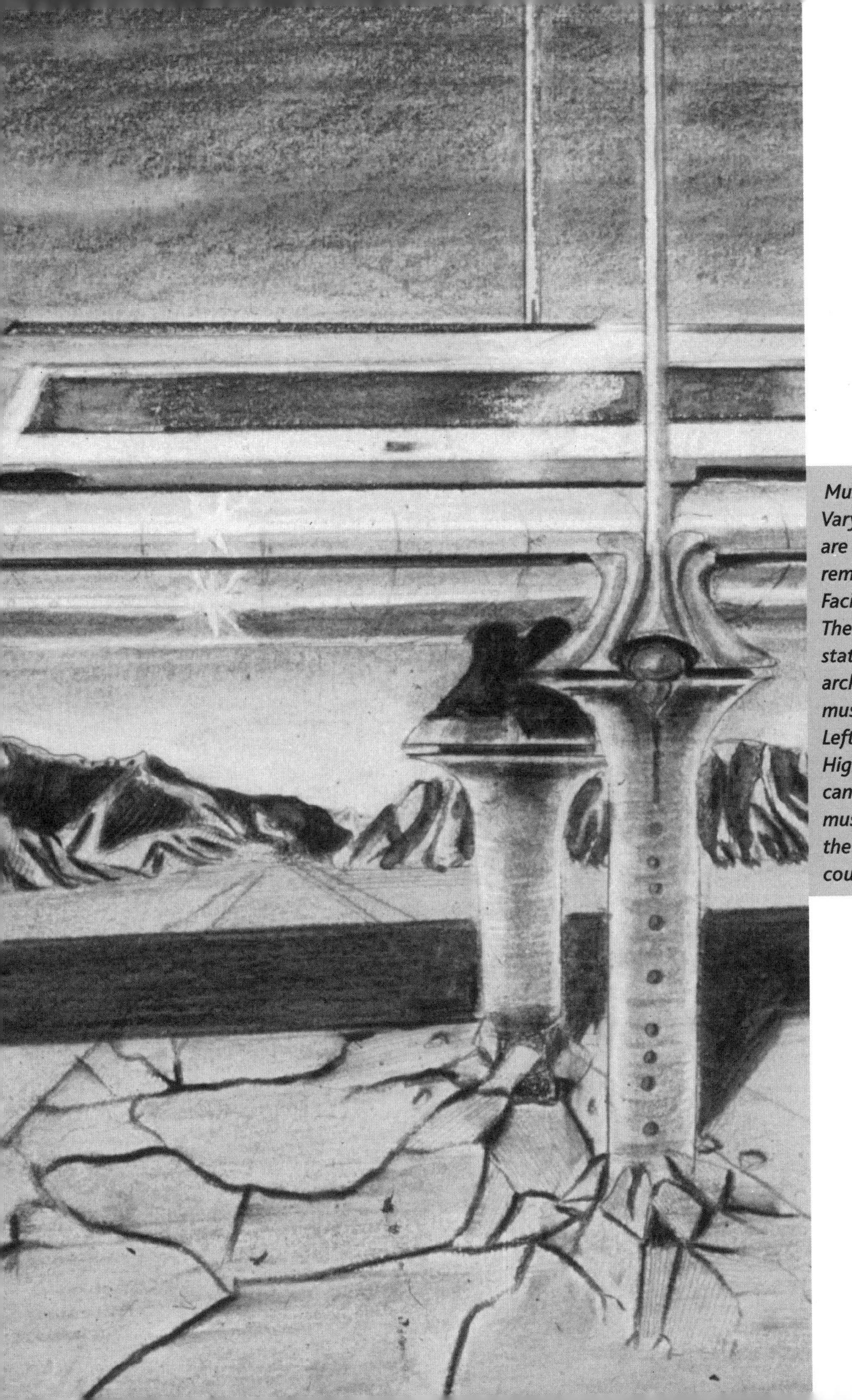

Museums of Varying Distances are delivered to remote places.
Facing page:
The railway station as an archaeological museum.
Left:
High-tech trains can transport the museum deep into the corners of the country.

ideas around which museum objects should be arranged?

I come now to the concluding part of this essay, which deals with speculation about future museums. We have to invent our future, not our past. The past is simply irrelevant as a model. The colonial invention of our past is now being overtaken by a newer invention that is being articulated by some rather fearful messengers who have seen the way to the paradise of Ramraj. What is perhaps relevant about the past are the various modes that once existed to acquire knowledge and skills. If these modes and skills are important to help us formulate our future, then they are relevant and important sources of inspiration as the contents of a museum.

In inventing our future and using museums to help us do so, two issues need to be tackled. First, what is the form of a future museum? Second, what are its contents?

The first future museum that I am proposing is the Museum of Varying Distances. The second is the Museum of Varying Amplifications. The Museum of Varying Distances is a means of delivering the museum exhibition to places of varying distances. It takes the display from a core vault location to a range of locations that has at its extreme end, the personal computer. So some of the delivery is done through, let us say, trains, while in other cases it uses the electronic medium and takes the exhibition into the house through the PC or broadcast channels.

The Museum of Varying Amplifications foresees museums where larger audiences participate or view objects or simulations or events in varying amplifications from, say, an audience of 500 to maybe 100,000, perhaps through simulations or mega-events. I am really exploring radical changes in the relationship between the creator of the object and the idea of the exhibition and the spectator. Something other than the nineteenth-century salon one, of one-to-one meditative relationship. This deep meditation of objects will no doubt continue, but it has already dominated museums for 200 years and there is no reason to assume that it will continue for ever.

It is possible to formulate these two museums. If we can leave behind the baggage of the last 200 years of European thought, then a beginning can be made. The Museums of Varying Distance and Amplification exist in two parts each. Each has a central core or vault as the secure location for objects. Exhibits from this location are withdrawn to illustrate creative ideas and taken to an outreach/outsource, which could be a room or a stadium or a huge landscape or even the whole island of Bali or a train.

The future museum is essentially a vehicle for new ideas: ideas that constantly explore frontiers, not transcendental ideas about our relative progress towards some utopia. In a way, I foresee an end to the belief in universality that the nineteenth century had given us, not only from European but also from Indian thinkers who had proposed reformations in religious outlook. We are no longer the guardians of ancient values and civilizations. We need to be the inventors of a future for ourselves, and the museum is a vital link in this project of inventing our future.

Montage image showing Jerusalem spinning out of control as the author sits on the Hill of Olives wearing a fool's cap and watching the sun go down.

The New Canaanites

Day after day alone on a hill
The man with a foolish grin
Is sitting perfectly still.
And nobody wants to know him
They can see that he is just a fool
For he never gives an answer
But the fool on the hill sees the sun going down
And the eyes in his head see the world spinning round.

Well on his way head in the clouds
The man with the empty mind is talking perfectly loud
But nobody seems to hear him
'Cause they think that he's just a fool,
And no one will quite go near him.

But the fool on the hill sees the sun going down,
And the eyes in his head see the world spinning round.

Round and round and round and round
He never listens to them.
He's no fool.

The Beatles

Throughout my eight months of wanderings in the beautiful landscape of Palestine it was difficult for me not to feel like a fool. Stepping across olive-grove terraces, brushing past shops in the narrow streets of Hebron and Jerusalem, or eating in cafeterias in the urban spaces of Tel Aviv, one was confronted by a reality that cannot make sense to a sane person. This tiny region has an importance that is quite out of proportion to its size. I could see at every turn only the approaching darkness of the setting sun. In this twilight I could see the place spinning out of control. The spin confused one at first. It seemed difficult to locate the starting-point of this spinning spiral. Every discussion, every argument, ended up against the wall with no space to place the first step towards unravelling the way out of the circular stagnation. Neither the Israelis nor the Palestinians will give an inch of concession. Whatever is given in discussions and reluctant, stiff handshakes in other countries abroad is taken back when the leadership returns home and addresses their fanatical groups. Netanyahu had not the slightest hesitation to withdraw from the national obligations agreed to in accords. I remember Clinton's visit to Palestine when he sat there in the council meeting of the Palestinians, praise being showered on him. The entire place, the roads and the parks, were decorated with American flags. The next day he returned to Washington and ordered

the bombing of Iraq. Palestinian students climbed the poles, ripped apart the flags and burned them. The Mayor of Bethlehem had been especially honoured by Clinton's presence at the Church of Nativity on Christmas eve. In the early hours of the morning he sent his staff to recover all the American flags on the streets. When the students demanded them later in the morning he agreed to let them burn the flags piled in a heap in the municipality premises.

The persistence in the search for a way to make some sense prevail only brought one in touch with or closer to other fools on the hill. Amira Hass was the first, the only Jew living in Palestine and bravely writing for an Israeli paper. Glen Bowman was another. Unable to keep away from Palestine, he spends all his time returning there to work his way deeper into the next layer of the dehumanizing conditions that prevail in the West Bank. Pilgrimages to Edward Said's talks were always well-rewarded. There were new ideas, new perspectives and an intensity of Palestinian passion that is rarely articulated so clearly by other Palestinians. The proposal for a train project presented here crystallized over many months of work in Jerusalem as well as extensive travels and interviews in Palestine and Israel. It was precipitated by Michael Sorkin's invitation to discuss it at a conference on Jerusalem in Bellagio.

Proposed train speeding through the landscape of New Canaan.

The most volatile wall in the world, its sides shared by Muslims and Jews in Jerusalem.
Above:
The inner side of the wall supports the garden soil around the Dome of the Rock.
Below:
The inner side of the wall – one of the most sacred of places for the Jews. They claim it as the remains of the western wall of the Second Herodian Temple and therefore the future base for the proposed Third temple.

In some ways the proposal at the end of this text is extremely ambitious. Not in its technical feasibility or its design quality. It is, in the end, only a train, with some rather special stations. The ambitiousness, then, is not part of the whoopee of architecture. The ambitions of the proposal are the ambitions attached to the thoughts of fools who see the possibility of another reality staring them in the face, a reality that is unavoidable to install in order to prevent the spiritual destruction and annihilation of one of the great power places of this world. The proposal is seen as an opportunity for the battered ship of modernism to dock at a port of call that could be reminiscent of its old yard where social concerns had welded its hull together. The proposal is of course a statement about modernism. Each station is a modern object, technically as well as spatially – a secular opening in the midst of the monopoly of all Jerusalem spaces by religious functions. It is part of a modern agenda that advocates an ideological reconstruct of the illusions and frustrated dreams that keep the Palestinians and Israelis apart. The proposed train, its routing and the stations along the way are placed as an assembled object in the centre of an ideological construct that proposes promotions, justice, integration and interdependence, rather than prevention, cruelty, the separation of apartheid and illusions of separate independences. The train proposes to resist the current forms of physical beatings and land thefts that at one time in the past were called exploitation and colonialism.

Another ambition of the project is the creation of an architecture of multilayered, multifunctional concourses. Religious fanatics could see the station concourse as a subversion of and resistance to their portrayals of space and time being exclusively religious in character and rhythm. The presence of the concourse and its many activities is the establishment of a secular space whose time and activities are regulated by the arrival of the trains. As passengers unload off these trains, the many activities in the concourse get activated. This is an alternative to the religious function of public space and the prayer rhythms of time in it that are part of the revalidation of ancient times which are inevitably defended with antagonism. The same space is claimed by different religions and each religious priest announces the same time as the time for prayers. Sundown in the plaza before the western wall is unforgettable, particularly on a Friday. As the orthodox Jews gather in a line in front of the wall, the muezzin begins his call to prayers from the minaret that dominates the wall. The Golden Dome of the Rock shines in the setting sun and the bells of the Church of the Holy Sepulchre begin their rhythmic tolling. Time in Jerusalem – daily time, festival time and annual time – is religious time.

Thus the proposal to locate Jerusalem Station at the edge of Damascus Gate is also seen as a counterbalance to the monopoly of

Site plan of the proposed Jerusalem Station

Israeli soldiers visit Masada, site of the ritual suicide by the Jews in defence against Roman occupation in AD 70.

space and time by the orthodox. It is the symbol of a new, secular future that confronts the predictions of ancient futurologists.

There is a wider ideological posture implied in the formulation of the proposal. This posture contends that significant modern proposals of architecture need to be placed in spaces where conflicts are destroying futures. That modern architectural proposals can lead to alternative solutions to hastily-sketched military ones. Military solutions diminish all other solutions and ideas. They forestall all efforts to probe any other than antagonistic dimensions. Even the most sophisticated and well-educated army remains ill-equipped to integrate. It is trained to disintegrate.

Modernism, for the moment, seems to have lost its ability to 'grow' in the advanced transatlantic regions. Corporate patronage, the collapse of the Soviet system, the disorientation of the left and the significance of environmental issues, have all contributed towards drying up the soil where modernism thrived so well at one time. Without ideological content, modernism in the advanced industrial areas of the world is just another profit-centre. The proposal therefore needs to be seen as a catalyst for reconciliation and reconstruction of an alternative future. Military solutions are regarded as the most destructive outcome of the technology of the modern state. Without having to articulate a new manifesto, the proposal's intentions are seen as interventions by a social democracy for the newly-emerging dual citizenship of the larger territory of Canaan. Its emphasis is not on securing nation-statehood but on formulation of common citizenships in the natural region of Canaan. Emergent potentials need to be seen in the context of geographical economies. I begin with explorations in history and the formulation of identities, and I argue that history is relevant to dormant potentials and not lost identities. Any emphasis on defining lost identities is seen as an antagonistic posture on the part of both the Palestinian and Israeli communities, and I dismiss it as having no relevance for a solution in the future.

The proposal assumes that the future of the region will be a dovetailed cohabitation of the populations of Palestine and Israel,

and eventually Jordan, in separate states, within a nation called
Canaan. It views these contiguous territories as one geographical and
economic region which the madness of colonial cartographic
divisions had disintegrated. The text looks at Edward Said's proposal
for reconciliation and the preconditions described by him. It proposes
alternatives to his views. His advocacy of the sharing of a common
history and education, and a syncretic citizenship of mergers of
identities, is questioned. Instead, my text proposes a shared economy
and the encouragement of a distinct character for each community.
It defines the dangers of defining identities and instead proposes
'character and potentials' as the creative source material which
needs development. I refuse to accept the viability of a separate
Palestine and Israel and argue that their gradual integration is the
only economically viable alternative to setting up two pretentious
Lilliputian national state economies.

Having discussed the regional context in terms of history,
geography and economics, the text goes on to Jerusalem, which is
the site of one of the train stations. History, geography and
economics are much denser factors in the decisions required to
define the future of Jerusalem. If Jerusalem is the third most holy city
for Muslims (after Mecca and Medina), it is also the first and last city
for Jews. Jews do not accept the earthly events that form the
narrative of Jerusalem. They do not accept easily that historical
events brought the Arabs to Jerusalem and kept them there for
centuries. The imposition of an imagined biblical history on the real
terrestrial history of Jerusalem inevitably leads to an antagonism
between celestially-ordained events and those that history and
archaeology explain. Arabs, for their part, do not recognize or accept
the powerful influence of the biblical narratives on the Jewish
imagination. This influence is etched in the memory of the Jews. It is
stirred and reinscribed with every ceremony and ritual. Zion is a
synonym for Jerusalem. When Theodore Herzl refined the concept of
a Jewish identity in Vienna at the end of the nineteenth century he
focused on Jerusalem, whose capture was fundamental to the
founding of a Zionist state. The national anthem of Israel, derived

from an early hymn, defines the Jewish dream – 'to be free in the land of Zion and Jerusalem'. Israel is not mentioned. Anybody sitting on a hill and watching Jerusalem 'spin out of control' would advocate reconciliation. There is a long list of writers who have passionately appealed to both sides to integrate themselves into a single nation composed of two provincial states. Almost all the material within this text has been considered by the proponents of reconciliation. This project, therefore, is not unique in advocating reconciliation. It only changes the emphasis and insists that political and territorial reconciliation needs a far deeper economic logic, and that it cannot spring from abstract notions of peace and accords. The underlying logic of economic integration enriches generations of inhabitants and creates a vested interest amongst the participating communities. Enrichment and development are greater incentives than military treaties. Round-table conferences of military advisors and the territorial fragmentations that get agreed upon are retrograde ways to build futures because they are invented by military experts as pretensions to everlasting peace.

Pilgrimage to Edward Said

The Palestine Exploration Fund was an unknown institution to most people I met in Palestine. Journalists, academics, social workers, even historians, were unaware of its existence. Understandable, considering that it is located in London. One journalist remarked to me that it had been founded by the Zionists to steal the past of the Arabs. I chanced upon its existence in a conversation with Veronique Dauge, a French archaeologist who was manning the UNESCO desk in the West Bank. Having completed an eight-month mission with the Ministry of Education of the Palestinian Authority, I went in search of it. Walking up Oxford Street, past the two shopping temples of Selfridges and Marks and Spencer's, one still had to ask the way to Hides Mews, an insignificant cul-de-sac off Marylebone Lane. A small dull green door with an unpolished visiting card-sized brass plate marked the location of the PEF. Felicity Cobbing, the curator, met me on the tiny landing. I still had a step to go to reach her level and I hesitated, wondering whether there was room enough for both of us to converse on that landing. She sat me down in the library, lined with books and filled with a large table and chairs ready to receive scholars or perhaps the board for its annual meeting.

'I'm sorry, I didn't catch your name on the phone. What exactly were you looking for?' Felicity was a young, fast-food-plump, very English archaeologist, whose glow and tan informed you about immense enthusiasm and many days spent at digs in the desert. My oriental caution immediately asserted itself in the tangential questions that I asked about the institution. Much later, with the bright yellow membership form still in my hands, I was able to be less tangential. 'Funded by the Zionists? Certainly not! We are quite well funded, thank you, and are one of the biggest landlords in this area, and our properties are out on commercial lets. Her Majesty, the Queen, is our patron, and the Archbishop of Canterbury is the president. Whatever gave you the idea that it was Zionist?'

The Palestine Exploration Fund was founded in 1865 by Christians to survey and map the Holy Land. From these maps, illustrators could travel to Palestine, discard the Arab names given to the ancient sites and make images that would inspire pilgrims to risk the arduous journey to all the sites associated with Christ's life. Pilgrimage would replace the enthusiasm and brutality of the Crusaders who had entered Jerusalem in 1099, slaughtered Muslims and Jews and called themselves 'armed pilgrims'. Gibbon called them 'savage heroes of the cross'. They massacred 50,000 Muslims and Jews in the narrow streets of Jerusalem and rode into the city triumphant, 'in blood up to their knees and bridle-reins'. Christian accounts of that armed pilgrimage frighten one – the thought that for half a year after the city had fallen to the Crusaders, it still 'reeked with the stench of rotting bodies'! Mercifully, the nineteenth-century desire for pilgrimage was tinted with romantic thoughts of the ancient cities of the Holy Land that David Roberts portrayed in the landscapes of the Sea of Galilee, Jerusalem, Bethlehem and others.

The badge of the PEF.

David Roberts' lithographs of *The Holy Land* created a new awareness of and attraction towards Jerusalem in the Christian world. No longer needing a crusade for liberation, this new image made the Holy Land a tourist attraction.
Above: Jerusalem
Below: Bethlehem

Some of the pioneering surveyors who went out to map the Holy Land and brave the attacks of 'those native brigands' were of course also scouts for the British expeditions that were going to mop up the peripheral reaches of the imploding Ottoman empire. Kitchner of Khartoum and T.E. Lawrence, both members of the Palestine Exploration Fund, were but two of the pawns in the great game that the British and the French would play out in the Near East. Surveying was always the precursor to occupation, as we discovered in India. These surveyors were a special breed and their trademark, the emblem and the badge of the PEF, was on the blazer-pockets of the members of the Fund.

My own explorations in Palestine were a series of simultaneous excursions. I was always acutely aware that I could not be anything other than a 'fool on the hill' watching the sun go down on this place, the eyes in my head seeing the place spinning out of control. Coming from a rich and wrinkled civilization that believes in polytheism, and whose spirituality and religion are encapsulated in multiple scriptures with multiple stanzas that abound in contradictions, I had been cast into a land where there was not the slightest trace of spirituality. There was one god all right and one book each for all the three faiths pivoted on Jerusalem, and there was religion too. But its power places were platforms of antagonism, claims and counterclaims. Sufis, I was told by the ministry architect, were 'people who entranced you and you can never work after that'. My long hair tied in a tail was regarded with extreme suspicion whenever I enquired about the spiritual places of Islam. The search had to begin somewhere else – the search for a solution that made sense to even a fool. It was not possible to accept that there was no way to stop the spinning.

I was driven to Nazareth by Amira Hass. The other passenger was Glen Bowman, an anthropologist teaching at the University of Kent, who has done enormous work on Palestine. Amira is Jewish, daughter of communist holocaust survivors, lives in Palestine and reports for the daily *Haaretz,* which comes out from Tel Aviv. We were on a pilgrimage to listen to Edward Said. The Anthropological

Association of Israel had invited him to speak at the annual
conference, on 'Borders and Beyond'. It was his first engagement
with an Israeli audience. Nazareth, the place of Christ's family, now
a bristling concrete forest crowned with a monster-building housing
the Israeli Courts of Justice, was hosting the conference.

Any reference to the places associated with Joseph and Mary
had been demystified long ago. At the site of the house of the
family there stood a massive cathedral with the upward-shooting
concrete beams of the nave. In a corner, under a slab supported by
columns, were the remains of a wooden table and some chairs.
'Joseph's Workshop', the sign announced. It was less painful to go to
the Meridien and glide about the marbled floors of the lobby to
register for the conference. Glen Bowman protested the high fee for
registration – even invited speakers had to pay to register. We
wondered whether Edward Said had to pay. He was the keynote
speaker at the conference. All the separate sessions were merged for
his talk. Partitions were folded back, chairs rearranged and
spotlights brought out. He stood floodlit on a platform too high for
that low basement ceiling in an L-shaped hall, facing a corner that
was protruding towards him. His divided audience, in flanks of chairs
to his left and right, was wrapped in silence. We could all see only
his profile. I recognized a few in the audience. Very few. They were
the exceptions who had heard Said speak some months earlier at
Birzeit University in the West Bank, whose students are considered
by some to be sympathetic to the Hammas.

Israel, Said said, is moving towards apartheid. Nobody in the
surrounding Arab region want the Palestinians. They are treated like
refugees in their own land and in the surrounding lands. In Egypt, he
explained, they have to report to the police every month. He
quoted Moshe Dayan as he continued: 'there is not one place in
Israel that did not have an Arab population'. He was less kind to the
Palestinians than he had been at Birzeit. The Palestinians persist in
dreaming about a pre-1948 situation coming back. The Israeli state,
in the meanwhile, is engaged in a campaign of misinformation,
which mops up all the 'space' that can be used for an alternative

Nazareth, the birthplace of Jesus Christ. The Basilica of the Annunciation erected over the grotto where Archangel Gabriel appeared to Mary.

view. Everybody distorts the future. He commented on how the Israeli military machine imposes a synthetic nationalism while Arafat continues to rule with the 'ludicrous trappings of a head of state'.

Amira and I looked at each other. His emphasis had changed since we had heard him at Birzeit. There had been much more of chest-beating at the Birziet engagement. We both understood the reason. It is so important in this land not to lose your audience. Softly, softly. 'Whatever happened to the common regional history of this place, perhaps the dialectics of separation is exhausted. . . . Now let us adjust to the disagreeable home that we have.' His message was clear: surrounded by tottering regimes and pulled and pressured by American exertions, this region had better find its own solutions from within its resources and communities. According to Said, the direction towards a common future was also clear. Quoting Raymond Williams, Said declared that the only hope lies in merging the separate identities of the Palestinians and Israelis into an 'emergent composite identity'. Said continued that it is imperative to merge the two histories of the region into a common one. One people, one history and a new composite future. According to him, the implied links between history and identity needed to be explored. The new emergent composite identity is clearly a syncretic one and requires, as a precondition, a sharing of the history of the two communities on the common land that they are trying to inhabit.

The question that seemed to remain unanswered was whether history is relevant for the formation of this new identity. It seemed to me, coming from a subcontinent of multilingual and multireligious identities, that Said's argument was advancing at sonic speed, assuming an unfolding of events that was beyond my comprehension. Glen Bowman, my fellow-passenger to Nazareth, had only just recently questioned the whole issue of identity formations as being destructive. But to that later. I looked at Glen as if to say, 'let's hear him out for now'. Said was appealing to the Palestinians to accept the connections between the historical and

Contemporary Palestine.
Above: Arafat in a postcard image flying over the Al Aqsa Mosque, evoking statesmanship and future dreams.
Below left: National parade in Ramallah, the future administrative capital of Palestine.
Below right: The devastated landscape of struggle and endless sacrifices of a stillborn nation that continues to be bled by its adversaries.

literary imperatives that had formed Israel and the role of the holocaust that had devastated the Jewish community in Europe. In turn, his appeal continued, the Jewish community must recognize that it perpetrated the *Naqba* of 1948 on the Palestinian community. I understood it as a kind of Desmond Tutu truth-and-reconciliation process that is needed to begin the healing process between Palestinians and Israelis. Many weeks later, with the innocence of the fool, I asked the Israeli architect Moshe Safdie whether the Holocaust and the *Naqba* could both be regarded as holocausts, and whether he thought that any reconciliation could begin by accepting the mutual significance of these events. '1948 was no holocaust', he replied. 'We lost millions of people in our holocaust.'

The word 'holocaust' has been appropriated into Israeli history and identity formation. Earlier dictionaries defined holocaust as 'a huge slaughter or destruction of life'. A later dictionary (Webster's) gives three meanings of holocaust: 1. 'A great or complete devastation or destruction.' 2. 'A sacrifice completely consumed by fire.' 3. 'The systematic mass extermination of European Jews in Nazi concentration camps during World War II.' I had thought that the *Naqba* had meant the complete devastation and destruction of Palestinian lives. From my position 'on the hill' I could barely make out the distinction between the cruelty that destroyed the Jewish community in five years and that which tortuously destroyed the Palestinian community over a period of fifty years. Moshe was not the only Israeli who protested against any comparison between the gas chambers and the refugee camps. But to me this was not the issue, nor was it the problem that needed to be resolved. Much more disturbing was how over fifty years had gone by since the Second World War and there had not been any development in human values, no forgiveness or acceptance of the sentiment that the spirit of man, battered in chambers and camps, needed time to heal.

By May 1945 there were perhaps 40 million uprooted people in Europe. About thirteen million Germans were expelled from the parts

of Germany annexed by Poland and the USSR, Czechoslovakia and
parts of southeastern Europe where they had long been settled. They
were taken in by the new Federal Republic of Germany which offered
a home and citizenship to any German who returned there, as the
new state of Israel offered 'a right of return' to any Jew.

Despite the enormous human catastrophes that had affected
both the Jews and the Palestinians between 1939–48, there seemed
no possibility to initiate something that could spark, between them,
even the thought of rapprochement after fifty years.

Said's impassioned plea for a common history needs a huge
mandate and a scale of scholarship and endeavour that may be
difficult to assemble in the time needed to slow down the suicidal
spin that Jerusalem and the region have got into. Dovetailing 5,000
years of archaeology, biblical texts and contemporary events into a
single joint seems very daunting. Only if the leadership of a society
conducts its affairs with some semblance of believing in the
principles that its scriptures proclaim is such an endeavour possible
– it requires an honesty that simply does not exist in either of these
two antagonized leaderships. History is used by both communities
as an important arsenal from which weapons are selected for the
ongoing simmering war between the Palestinians and the Israelis.
There are too many versions of the history of that region.
Archaeological evidence, religious texts and political agendas are
mixed and matched to create attractive patterns that bear no
resemblance to reality. How far back could I go to find a common
seed to the history of the region, which the two communities could
agree to share as a common beginning?

Clear as Sliding Mud on a Monsoon-Struck Mountain

With every book I read, every archaeological site I visited and every
religious text I ploughed through, the historical narrative of the
place was, I found, as clear as sliding mud on a monsoon-struck
mountain. I began, naturally, with the Canaanites, hoping that a
period of history before the formation of the Islamic and Jewish
histories could provide me with relatively stable conditions. The

Canaanites are said to be the original settled inhabitants of the region of Palestine, extending to the Levant. I naturally began my enquiries amongst Palestinian historians and writers. It was not as easy as walking into the library of the Palestine Exploration Fund with its century-old archives that have been meticulously preserved, and I am not a scholar of Arabic. Admittedly, I was trying to enter the race on crutches and, seeing my torment, Suad Aamiry handed me a thin volume that her father had written. Our meeting to discuss various ways to stop the commercial plunder of old Ramallah and the 'disasters of gentrification' had just concluded when she made her offer. In his work, *Jerusalem: Arab Origins and Heritage*, M.A. Aamiry, a distinguished Palestinian, states quite categorically that the pre-Islamic tribes of Palestine had migrated from the Arab peninsula. The Canaanites and Amarites had emerged out of Arabia and settled in the Levant as part of a process of migration. Coming from the desert-sands of Arabia, attracted by the fertile prosperity of the 'fertile crescent' that encompassed the ancient civilizations of Mesopotamia and Syria, these tribes are said to have been Arabic, thus concluding that the civilization and culture of the Levant, from ancient times, was an inseparable part of the Arab peninsula. 'The heart of Arabia was the cradle of the Arab race, the Fertile Crescent its area of development.'

Jonathan Tubb's book on the Canaanites places the whole matter in a different context that dismisses attempts to link the Canaanites to Arabia as 'dreamed up'. He says: 'In most basic terms, the Canaanites were the people who occupied the land of Canaan from time immemorial . . . it is broadly possible to equate ancient Canaan with the modern state of Israel, Trans-Jordan coastal Syria (including Lebanon) and southern inland Syria.' Armed with the logical and methodological approach that emerged with the establishment of modernism in Europe in the last century, Tubb has the backing of the British Museum, where he is the curator of the section on Syria-Palestine within the West Asiatic Department. He is an expert on Levantine archaeology. Despite his authoritative dismissal of the Arab origins of Canaanite culture, he had to face

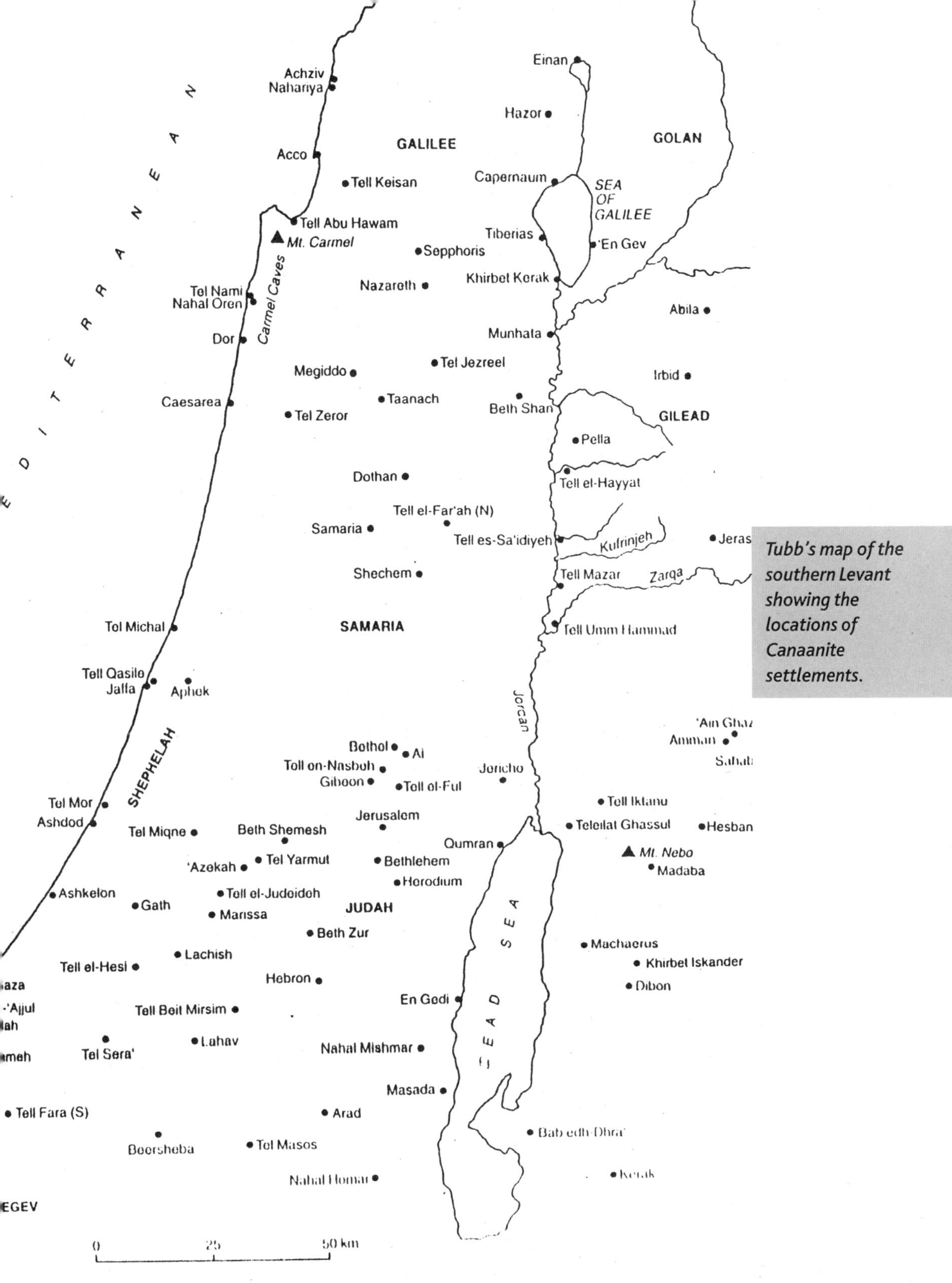

Tubb's map of the southern Levant showing the locations of Canaanite settlements.

historiographic hurdles which had to be sidestepped. 'In the case of the Canaanites, the absence of contemporary textual data means that by necessity the type of historical reconstruction presented in the book is rather different and may seem by comparison somewhat sparse . . . it has been considered appropriate to admit material drawn from biblical narratives.'

The difficulty of admitting these narratives as historical evidence made me smile. The Books of Joshua and Judges depict the land of Canaan as 'the Promised Land' to which the Israelites were to return to settle after defeating the local inhabitants. The Book of Joshua opens with the Lord's instructions to Joshua: '. . . go over this Jordan, you and all this people, into the land which I am giving to them, to the peoples of Israel. Every place that the sole of your foot will tread upon I have given to you.' And later, '. . . without fail drive out from before you the Canaanites, the Hittites, the Hivites, the Perizittes, the Gir'gashites, the Amorites and the Jebusites.' Joshua did as his Lord told him to. He took

> all the land, the hill country and all the Negev and all the land of
> Goshen and lowlands and the Arabah and the hill country of Israel
> and its lowland. . . . And he took all their kings and smote them and
> put them to death . . . it was the Lord's doing . . . that they should be
> utterly destroyed and should receive no mercy, but be
> exterminated. . . .

Reconstituting any narrative in ancient history is akin to crossing a swamp by jumping from stone to stone. The place one lands up at the other end depends on which stones were stepped on. *Terra firma* is certainly not visible. Defining an ancient origin and narrative that the Muslims and the Jews would agree to share will probably have to await the Day of Reckoning despite Tubb's assertion that 'the Israelites were themselves Canaanites'. A coincidence of ancestry cannot help weave the descendants of Ismail and Isaac into the strands of a common story. The ironies of history will keep knotting up the effort.

In the British Museum a new gallery has been set up for the

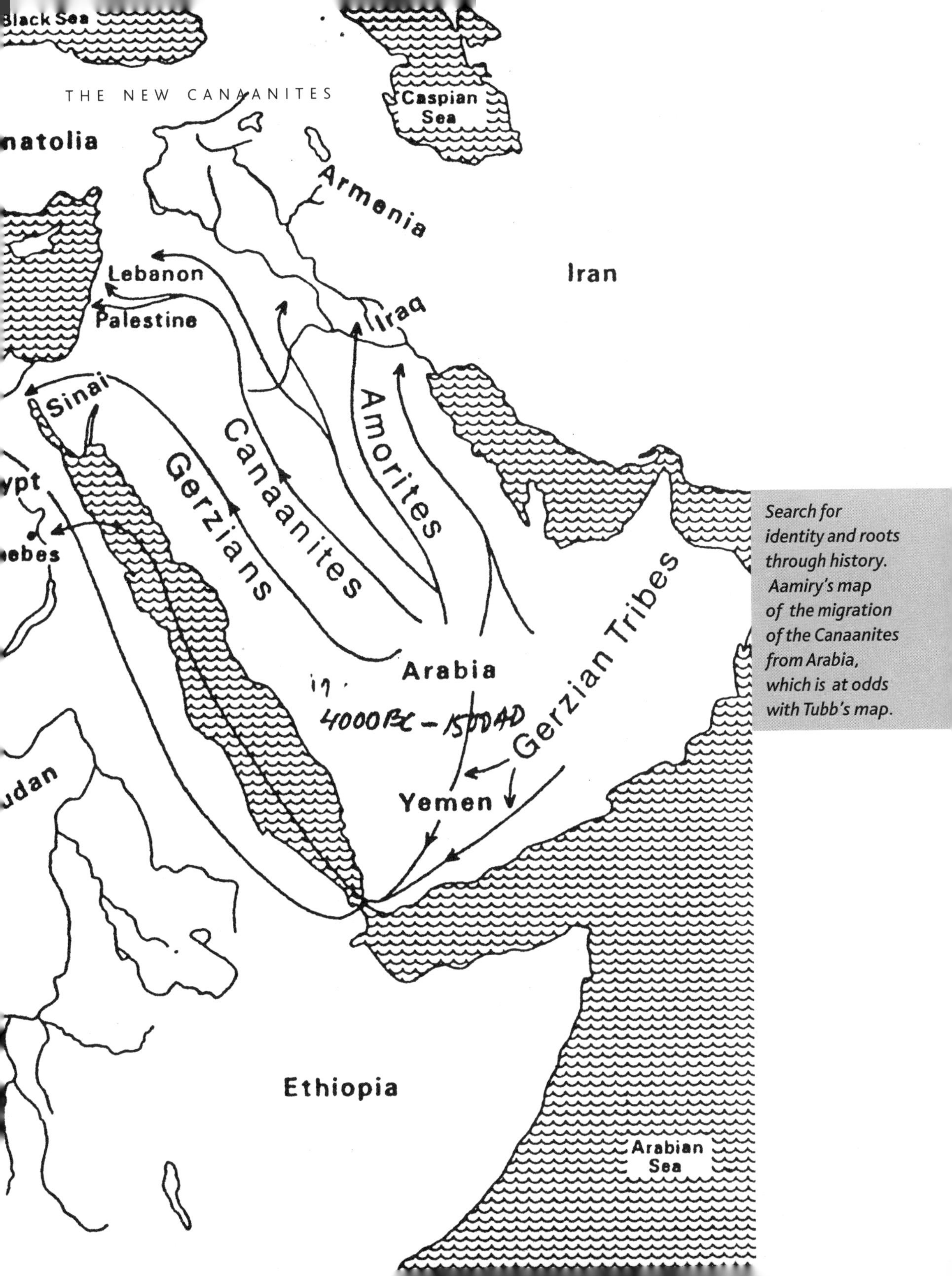

Search for identity and roots through history. Aamiry's map of the migration of the Canaanites from Arabia, which is at odds with Tubb's map.

Levant through donations from the Sackler family. Alongside one of the showcases displaying the polytheistic figurines of the Levant, the text printed on the wall mentions a people called the Hapiru. First discovered in the text of the Babylonian Amara clay-tablet letters to the Pharaoh, the Hapiru are described as 'lawless groups of bandits, criminals and social misfits'. The princes of the outer reaches of the Pharonic empire described them as 'dispossessed and homeless people'. The word Hapiru later became Hebrew. All Hebrews are Hapirus but all Hapirus are not Hebrew. Leaving aside the question of the origin of the Canaanites, the divergence that begins to manifest between the biblical narrative and archaeological evidence will not be acceptable to the Jewish community, to whom the Exile and the Exodus are such emotional components of identity. One could argue that economic development, industrial progress, scientific thought and belief in empirical evidence could always be relied on to weaken the collective belief in a mythical past. My own fanatical countrymen, though, can never be persuaded to deny the existence of characters from the epics who established powerful kingdoms, for which there is not a shred of archaeological evidence. But then we are regarded in the west as part of the third world, clutching insecurely to a mythical past because a contemporary future seems so bleak in the face of growing poverty and the supremacy of the North Atlantic. But that the inhabitants of the modern western industrialized state of Israel should clutch on to its invented origins despite evidence to the contrary is somewhat curious.

Cooking 'origins' in the furnace of history as an ingredient in the identity recipe seems to deeply satisfy some emotional need. It would take a rather brave citizen of Israel to openly accept other than a Jewish identity for the state of Israel. One European view explains that the Israelites were a socio-political group that was rendered homeless when the Egyptian empire's rule over the Levant declined. These dispossessed and homeless people were forced to migrate to the hills of Judaea and Samaria, where they established themselves as small farming communities who then became known as Hapirus to the Egyptians. So the identity of the Israelites was formed in the same hills as was the identity of contemporary Palestinians. The wrinkles of history are difficult to iron out. One needs the strength of a mullah or a rabbi to hold the hot iron. Such a theory of Israelite origin creates enormous conceptual problems for important narrated events such as the Exodus. Tubb candidly declares: 'The results of archaeological research have, in a sense, compounded the problems, for they have demonstrated that the story of the Exodus is no longer required in order to explain the birth and growth of the Israelite Nation.'

Last November, Ze'er Herzog, a professor of archaeology at Tel Aviv University, published an article in *Aa-aretz.* He wrote:

> the Israelites were never in Egypt, did not wander in the desert, did not conquer the land in a military campaign and did not pass it on to the twelve tribes of Israel. Perhaps even harder to swallow is that the united monarchy of David and Solomon, which is described in the Bible as a regional power, was at most a small tribal kingdom.

Although the Palestinians have been concerned about their origin, it is not a matter that exercises their minds greatly. They are quite happy to splash about in the large pool of Arab nationalism, knowing that the question of origin is also one of concern to the twenty-two other countries which share with them an Arab identity. For Israel, as we have seen, it is an entirely different matter. When a nation is formed in contemporary times by gathering together flocks of communities whose colour, language and culture are international, and when this nation wants to use ancient biblical texts to forge a single synthetic identity, then inevitably there are problems. Events like the Exodus and the Holocaust are vital instruments in the forging of a single identity. The contemporary state of Israel needs an imagined history as a single undisputed narrative to overcome the deep differences within a community which originated in Central and East Europe (Ashkenazi), Spain, Portugal, the Mediterranean basin and Maghrel (Sephardi), Yemen, Ethiopia, Afghanistan, Iran, Iraq, India and Central Asia, in over 80 countries. Moshe Safdie assured me twice that these differences did not matter to the Jewish community and that the second generation of migrants was already comfortable with inter-marriages, which were a common occurrence. But I come from a land of linguistic and cultural differences and Moshe's assurances had little persuasion. That evening the Likud Party announced its candidates for the election and a group of Moroccan Jews created enormous disorder, yelling in protest against the conspiracy to keep them out of representation. Intermarriages seemed like thin pieces of tissue pasted over deep cracks.

The state of Israel is uncomfortable with archaeology and 'the results of digs are seldom ever published', Veronique Dauge from the UNESCO in Palestine informed me. This is quite understandable and I remembered what Felicity had said at the Palestine Exploration Fund: 'Oh, we do our excavations in Jordan. It just isn't right somehow in Israel.' The Jews in Israel have travelled too far on the route laid out from an imagined past to an imagined future. It is difficult to retrace this route and attempt to follow Said's advice. Consider the enormous importance given by the Jews to their first king, David, and to the founder of their temple, Solomon, and compare this to the comment of an archaeologist:

> The opulent empire founded by David and developed by Solomon seems to have left no trace whatsoever in the archaeological record . . . the material culture of the initial phase of the 'Israelite' Iron Age, although clearly derived from the Canaanite culture of the late Bronze Age, is remarkable only for its extreme impoverishment and lack of aesthetic sensibility. It is important to look at the biblical texts, and to appreciate that they were not written, or at least edited, until at least 400 years after the events they refer to. At this time, perhaps during the exile, the motivation of their composition was surely to create an historical 'golden age', a past glory which would give hope and inspiration to the exiles.

This comment questions the status of the First Temple as a significant aesthetic structure. Archaeologists hint at a temple excavated as a structure which had been built on top of the remains of the Egyptian governor's palace in Tell es-Saidiyeh, a place located along the Jordan river halfway to the Sea of Galilee from Jericho. This is the only temple that has been found that was contemporary to the time of David and Solomon (997–930 BC). It has been described as 'a small and poorly preserved building which is believed to be a type of temple'. For the contemporary state of Israel to consider that the First Temple could have been located in any place other than Jerusalem would need enormous persuasion. The basis for the Israeli claim on Jerusalem today is that it was the site of the first two temples. It is much more pertinent for Israel to assert that the remains of the First Temple lie buried under the foundations of the Second Temple whose enormous size, represented so picturesquely in the Tower of David Museum, could easily obscure earlier remains.

Disregarding the absence of archaeological evidence clearly strengthens the Palestinian refutation of Jewish claims on the Haram Sharif site. Aamiry explains in his book that the kingdom of David lasted barely 70 years, after which the Jews were dispersed – hardly the basis for establishing a claim on Jerusalem where Muslims have lived in continuous occupation for 1,100 years. History cannot be shared. If history cannot be shared, then Said's appeal to share a common educational programme also cannot materialize in the foreseeable future. Nor can the Jewish community be expected to give up the symbolism of the holocaust and share their disaster with that which befell the Palestinians in 1948. In Palestine as well as in Israel, Yuri Lotman's contention holds validity. The intellectual history of both nations can be examined as a struggle for memory. Every destruction of the Palestinian and Jewish cultures has been accompanied by a destruction of memory, erasure of texts and obliteration of links. With each new cultural formation, both communities have selectively reconstructed their memories and formulated new identities with the help of new struggles and antagonisms. For both communities, even a fool can see, this is a disastrous and self-

Pre-1967 view of Arab houses adjacent to the western wall in Jerusalem. These were bulldozed in a rapid action attack to clear the space for the western wall plaza. This marked the beginning of a new phase to claim the Temple Mound.

destructive process. The formation of imagined identities through references to historical holocausts must perforce rely on aggressive stances because the very definition of each identity is a fiction that confronts the other through violence. The one, the Arab community, irrevocably bitter at having lost the wars in which their fellow Arabs eventually abandoned them; the other, the Israeli community, armed to the teeth, vowing never to be incarcerated in ghettos ever again. The bloodstreams of both communities are poisoned with a virus. This virus has eaten away the spirit, the soul and all else inside a human being that carries it forward. The souls of both communities lie poisoned. A poisoned soul cannot confront the enemy. It is pertinent here to recall a Buddhist text which tells us: you have to be a warrior in life and a warrior has truth on his side, and there is only one truth – that which emerges from compassion.

Of the many propositions advocated by Edward Said, it still needs to be seen whether it is possible to gain a reconciliation between the Palestinians and the Israelis by making efforts to form an 'emergent composite identity' – a kind of secular suprahistorical new citizen. It seems, on the face of it, a fine intellectual concept but, as I hope to argue later, it is one that will further aggravate the situation. Identity is an altogether more recent manipulated phenomenon in nation-building. The construction of the present Palestinian and Israeli identities is linked irrevocably to the imaginations of the diaspora of both communities. It is a contemporary concept that has been synthetically forged as an aggressive defence mechanism, and is hence drenched in blood and tears.

Any efforts at reconciliation would need to consider Bakhtin's theoretical concept rather than the concept advocated by Edward Said which, as I have explained, is hazardous. Bakhtin's concept is a theoretical definition and is not related in any way to either the Palestinians or the Israelis. He explains that in each culture the past has enormous characteristics and potentials which remain hidden, unrevealed and unrealized. These are present throughout the history of that culture. One culture discovers itself through the eyes of the

other. The presence of an alien adjacent culture inevitably leads to
new questions being asked about itself. The alien culture too views
the neighbouring culture as a whole, an entity, and the portrayal of
it as such informs that neighbouring culture about itself. Newer and
deeper meanings begin to be discovered about the identity of both
cultures. The ensuing dialogue between the two cultures does not
result in a merger or mixture or blending of the two into one. Each
culture retains its unity and uniqueness and both cultures get
enriched. Each culture reinforces its own integral nature. Said's
proposition for a new syncretic citizen emerging out of this region
seems unrealizable. The quest for reconciliation is therefore the
quest for a formation of two separate potentials, each unique but
dependent on the other for the realization of that potential.

Such a process cannot be established easily. It can only be
commenced with a bold intervention that forcibly halts the current
trajectories being followed for creating identities that have no
conceivable relevance to the future. The project explained at the
end of this text is a proposal for such an intervention. It is too neat
to talk about identity formation. There is something unavoidably
attractive about the concept of identity. It is a smooth way to
counter the new internationalism and global homogenization but it
is fraught with problems, as Glen Bowman has so eloquently
described in his paper, 'Exile Imagination', which he delivered at the
Birzeit University seminar on Landscapes.

Glen is a quiet professional anthropologist. Throughout most
of the journey he sat at the back of the car without uttering a word,
listening to my tirades of impatience with the Palestinian Ministry
of Education. As I paused for breath he uttered a single sentence:
'You have a very orientalist attitude. I'm not sure I approve of it.'
Amira just smiled and drove on, saying, 'Glen, you'll get to know
him.' Amira's parents were communists and holocaust survivors
from the Balkans. She speaks Arabic, travels regularly to Tel Aviv to
her paper's office and avoids using her phone as much as possible.
We were three characters racing in a small car through the beautiful
olive groves of Palestine, searching for a better way to define the

Children sifting through the sands of time at an archaeological site of ancient Canaan. Archaeology and the interpretation of its findings in Israel have become linked to the search for Jewish roots in the ancient texts. Israeli archaeologists seldom publish their findings in international journals.

future of this land, listening to pundits of the social sciences at seminars. Glen's paper deals primarily with the construction of the identities of the Palestinian and Israeli peoples. It seemed to me crucial to consider the question of identity construction if one has to examine Said's concept of formulating an emergent composite identity. Bakhtin's alternative idea of developing the separateness of each identity as the basis of a syncretic relationship had a strong attraction. As a detached, partially-informed fool on the hill, I could sense the essentially synthetic quality of new composite identities. It hadn't worked in my part of the world and I could not see how it could succeed in Palestine. The identities of both the Palestinians and the Israelis are closely tied to their imagined image of the territory that constitutes the 'homeland' of both peoples. In both cases this image, Bowman contends, has been formulated in an external place, either in exile or in the minds of Jews who imagined it long before they came to the land. The land and the indigenous communities who never left the land have therefore been forced to accept this imagined identity of the landscape which, in reality, bears little resemblance to the ground realities of what was once Palestine. In the case of the Palestinians, the resident community which was saved from exile has been forced to accept the imagined identity that the Palestinian Authority (ruled by the returnees) has imposed on them. The imagined reality of the exiles is not an embroidery-on-the-wall memory of their land. It is symbolized in the exercising of, what Said terms, the ridiculous trappings of state power. In the case of the Israelis, the resident community of what now constitutes the state of Israel has been forced to accept the overarticulated but completely invented identity of Israel. It is this invented identity that Amira Hass refuses to accept and her vehement opposition to it has caused her to dwell among the Palestinians.

Lasting reconciliation needs to be based on issues which are real and which arise out of the everyday life of the land and its economy. It cannot be dependent on the construction of an imagined identity, linked to the embroidery on the walls of diaspora rooms and biblical narratives, or on the ridiculous and expensive gestures by which both the Palestinian Authority and the Israeli government pretend that they have each inherited a viable nation-state that can exist in isolation of the other. Bowman's contention that the quest for identity *per se* is a reductionist quest has obvious validity. Such a quest has left both the communities poorer in terms of ignoring the potentials of mutual dependence:

> When one calls something an identity, one is already fetishizing, picking elements out of that wider range of sociability, that general range of action that people engage in, that very diffused sense of everything one does in the course of one's everyday life. One is – in articulating an identity – pulling out the dense fabric of interwoven elements certain figures, certain symbols, activities, entities that serve as vehicles for saying 'this is who we are!' These are metonyms – parts which come to stand for the whole – and to comprehend identity, we need to understand such processes of abstraction and reduction.

Reconciliation proposals must therefore move closer to Bakhtin's notions of *character* and *potential* rather than articulation of identities. Articulation of identities and their fictional construction in any form is a regressive way to move to the future. If the character and potential of a community are threatened it reacts very quickly by reconstructing its identity – usually from the debris of the past. In this reconstruction it must assume antagonistic modes that eventually justify separation and conflict. Conflict galvanizes identity construction and ignores potential and character as the more obvious building-blocks of the future. Glen Bowman argues further: 'Antagonism is fundamental to the process of fetishization which underlies identity . . . identity terms come into usage at precisely the moment in which . . . one comes to feel that they stand in for a being or an entity one has to fight to defeat.'

Unfortunately, both the Palestinians and the Israelis have continued to give the highest priority to identity construction. This has at its core an expression of mutual antagonism – the harsher the definition of the other, the more intense is the feeling of righteousness and the clearer defined are the edges of identity construction. There may be good reasons for this. Since 1948 the Palestinians have been threatened by what they perceive as extermination at the hands of an Israel armed to ridiculous levels of preparedness. The Jews on their part have experienced, in the holocaust, attempts at their extermination. For the Palestinians the construction of identity is relatively recent. They do not need to become obsessed with the issue of origin that characterizes the rituals and literature of the Jews. Palestinians are comfortable to share the Arab dream with the Arab world; they know that they have been in continuous occupation of the land from ancient times and, being a homogeneous community, they do not concern themselves with doubts about their origins. For them, identity means an imagined statehood and a road that fulfils the Arab dream. When the Arab singers all got together and sang the 'Arab Dream' in a 'We are the World' fashion, every Palestinian knew the words. For over a month channels in Syria, Oman, Egypt, Jordan, Saudi, Dubai, Palestine and Lebanon telecast videos of the song. It seemed to have captured the imagination of every Palestinian I met. Amidst the chorus singing

> Generation after generation
> Will live our dream . . .
> Maybe the darkness of night
> Will keep us apart today
> But the rays of light will reach
> The furthest sky

singer after singer from the various Arab countries took the microphone and sang stanza after stanza:

> This is the dream of our lifetime
> A body to embrace us all.

Speak with all your strength
Even if the world is against you
The thousand-mile journey
Starts with the first step on the road.
Stand firm, confront the universe,
Protest and learn to be courageous.

Justice needs power to be protected.

From any place on earth,
Wherever people speak Arabic
We declare with our loudest voices
And heartbeats
'This unity is our new birth.'
All the locked roads
Will be opened by the power of love.
Songs eliminate borders and
Dwell deep in the heart.

And love isn't just words,
But deeds and sensations.
Our dream at all times
Is the Unity of all our lands.
All the disputes will disappear
And the humanity in you will prevail.

If the Palestinian dream is to become united with the Arab world without blocked roads, the Israeli dream is to establish Eretz, or a land of Zion, on the same territory. Liberal Israelis argue that such a dream is confined to militant orthodox Jews, but in the current atmosphere of aggression it is the Zionist ambition that observers like me perceive as the driving motivation for the presence of young Israeli soldiers armed with oversized automatics at every street-corner and the humiliating interrogations at the airport. The land is being defended at every moment in every space. Clearly, the Jews have had a much longer history of experiencing extermination. Their whole narrative is built, it seems, around notions of exile, exodus and return to the land. The very formulation of Jewishness and Israel has been hammered into an identity emerging out of extermination threats.

The destruction of Jerusalem in 586 BC by the Babylonian king Nebuchadnezer and the exile of the so-called Israeli tribes to Babylon is narrated as the first-ever perceived threat to the community as a whole. This period of the first exile could therefore be considered as the first significant antagonism that the Jews experienced. They responded to this by forming the concept of an Israeli identity which they said was given to them by Moses, who received the commandment on Mount Sinai. The return to the land of Samaria and the encouragement of antagonisms to justify the return are peppered all over the Old Testament. Their persecution continued during the rule of the Roman empire: the Second Temple too was destroyed and then there was the legendary mass suicide incident of the mountain-top Masada being exterminated by the Romans.

Another period of collective persecution that the Jews faced was much later in the Middle Ages, when the Crusaders marched into the land. Just as the first antagonisms of exile were used to galvanize the Jewish identity, so the confrontation with the Christians was used to further identify the special character of Jewishness. The first exile split the Israelites from their common Canaan ancestors, and the Crusaders split them from their common Canaan neighbours, the Christians. In both cases the split was defined as a major historical catastrophe that helped harden the edges of Jewish identity. The sharing of a common spiritual descent from Adam, Eve, Abraham and Moses could not provide any sense of a shared origin during the period after Christ. The Christian accounts in the New Testament of the treatment given to Christ after Pilate's hearing clearly lets off the Roman governor lightly and places the responsibility for the crucifixion on the Jews. When Pilate asks the crowd and the priests, 'whom do you want me to release for you, Barab'bas (a notorious prisoner) or Jesus who is called Christ?', the chief priests and the elders persuade the people 'to ask for Barab'bas and destroy Jesus'. And when Pilate washes his hands and declares his innocence of responsibility, the people answer, 'His blood be on us and on our children!'

The Latin Crusaders struck Jerusalem in AD 1099 and devastated the orthodox Christian, Muslim and Jewish populations. The main mosques were stripped of their Islamic symbols and the Dome of the Rock, claimed as the sacred site of the two Jewish temples, was transformed from an Islamic mosque to a Christian church. The formation of the Jewish identity was thus moulded not only by a series of persecutions but also by schisms – first the split with the polytheistic Canaanites leading to the emergence of a monotheistic religion recognizing only Yaweh-Alone, and then the split with the Christians. This was followed, much later in the nineteenth century, by the invention of the idea of Zionism – the intellectual creation of Theodore Herzl, who is regarded by the Jews as the father of the state of Israel. Herzl, in a sense, drew the intellectual boundaries within which the Jews could be defined in the twentieth century. Unable to be accepted in Viennese circles and rejecting therefore the universalism and enlightenment of mid-nineteenth-century Europe as a person being discriminated against, Herzl reacted by defining a new nationalism for the Jews and called it Zionism. He advocated a separatism that would culminate in a demand for a separate state outside Europe. The idea of locating such a state in Palestine had begun and so had the strong reaction against it. Pius X in 1894 told Herzl that

> Jerusalem must not fall into the hands of the Jews, who denied Christ and still deny him. The Hebrews have never recognized our land. Therefore we cannot recognize the Hebrew people and should they persist in their desire to return to Palestine we shall keep churches and priests ready to baptise all of them.

Every stage of the formation of the Jewish identity was marked by a response to antagonism, and the Jews reacted with counter-antagonism. Thus was formed the modern state of Israel, and thus was formed the character of the citizens of that state.

Beyond Edward Said

Moving beyond the possibilities of finding a common ground from where one can discuss the possibilities of reconciliation in history and of identities, I turn to the concluding portion of my argument, which deals with a possible future scenario for this land. It is my contention that it is not possible to follow any of the leads given by Edward Said in his lecture at Nazareth because they are based on an abstract intellectual idea that does not enable moving forward beyond the elementary problems imposed by an imagined history on both communities. The alternative history that archaeology can put together is already compromised by the reliance on biblical texts to perform the giant leaps in time that are needed to connect the evidence from digs. I would like to argue that Bakhtin's notion of dovetailing the separate character and potential of the Palestinians and Israelis into a more stable mutual interdependence is the only way out. The economic sector is the only area in the lives of these two nations that can provide a realistic state of interdependence. It is this sector that is proposed as providing a context in which rapprochement can be considered and in which the world community can participate. Within this economic sector, a proposal is made for a specific modern intervention – a train and its stations that are defined as new catalysts for change. The train as a project proposal is seen as a solution not only for Jerusalem but for the region as a whole. It is seen as the meeting-line where mutual interdependence can begin. It discounts the role of identities and proposes character and potential as the basis for moving forward.

The economic wealth of the divided territories of Palestine can be harnessed and accumulated for the benefit of the people only if the entire land is viewed as a composite whole and considered to be an integrated territory. Within it there are component production areas which are interdependent. It is not, in my view, possible for either Israel or Palestine to exist as stand-alone nations. I hope to show, as my argument proceeds, that the current modes of production and exchange of commodities being practised in the land are governed solely by antagonism between the two communities. It is the tragedy of this region that its economy is regulated by military dictates rather than market forces. No amount of a semblance of democracy in Israel can conceal the parasitic laws that the Israeli military has arbitrarily imposed on Palestine. It is difficult to believe that an Israeli who lives and enjoys European standards of living within his state is unaware of the growing poverty and unemployment being imposed on his neighbours, the Palestinians, by the military of his state. The Israeli economy is attempting to define its identity through antagonism and isolation, and is ignoring the vital interdependence that the hill regions share with the coastal plains and deserts of Israel.

The Oslo Accord has been accepted by the Palestinian National Authority which, as we have seen, is ruled by returnees with dreams of ruling over a nation-state. This accord has reduced the unified territories of Palestine into an archipelago of reservations between which peoples and goods may travel at the pleasure of Israeli troops, should it please them to permit this movement. Sitting in a cell of the Ministry of Education office that I had set up in Ramallah, I was warned one day to quickly evacuate the office. Ramallah is one of the urban territories that was vacated by the Israeli troops under the Oslo Accord, and the PNA controls its security. I was a little slow in running down the floors, more concerned with turning off the computers which the staff had abandoned with such alacrity. By the time I got down and out of the building bullets were already ricocheting between buildings. A line of helmeted Israeli soldiers was advancing at a quick pace, firing from the waist. Shielding my head with my briefcase, which contained some large volumes of statistics hopefully thick enough to divert a bullet, I ran in the opposite direction, dodging behind parked cars, some of whose windscreens had shattered. The staff of the office was waving to me from behind a large building and I waited it out there with dozen colleagues. We were able to return when armoured cars came and evacuated the troops. Bullets lay on the floor of the office, the glass was completely shattered. They

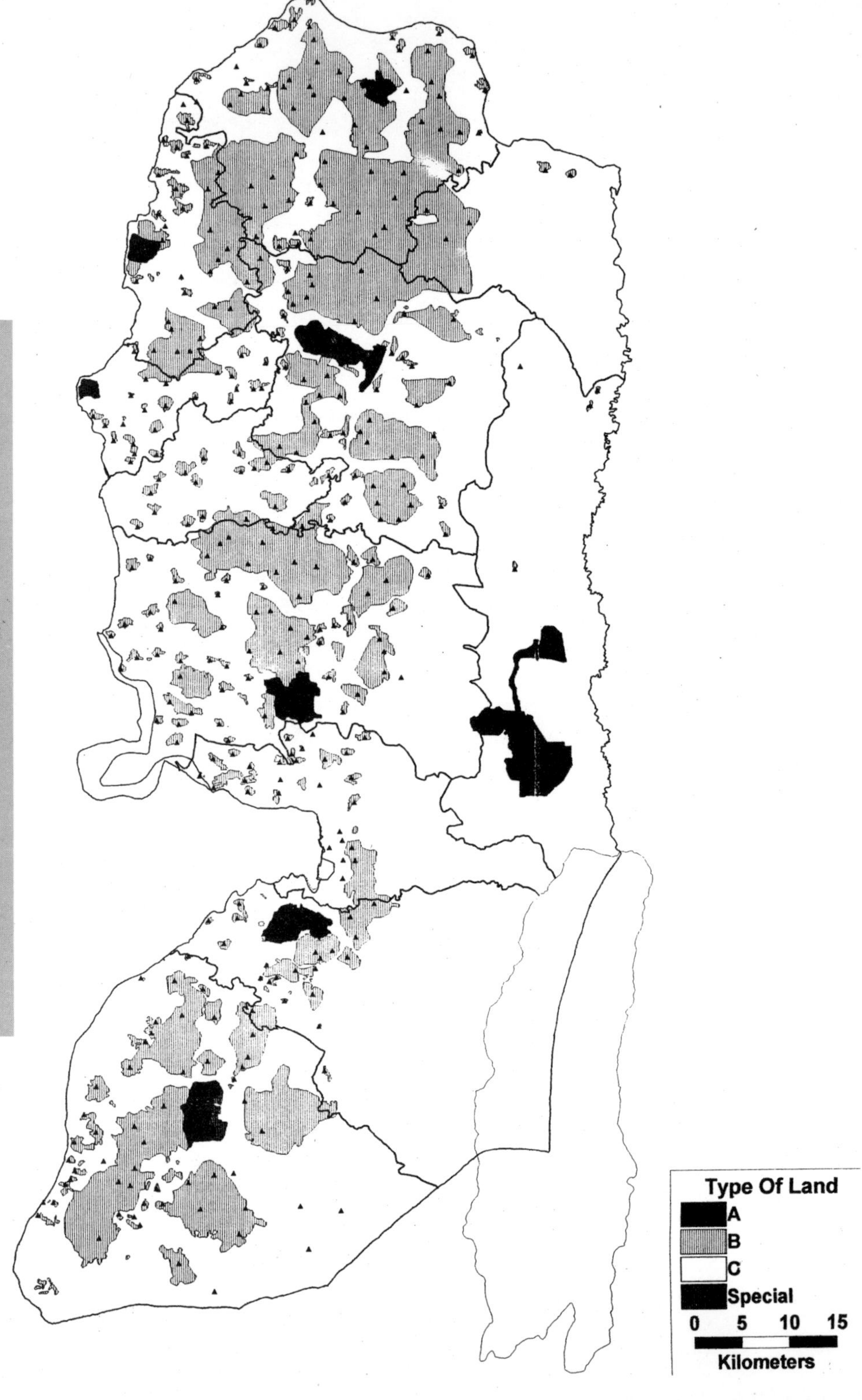

The struggle for survival in Palestine is aggravated by the cruelty of maps and the arbitrary divisions marked on them. The infamous Oslo Accord, signed in 1993, divided the Palestinian land into A, B and C territories. The Palestinians were given a license to control administration only in the A territories. It is a license that can be withdrawn at any time.

Type Of Land
A
B
C
Special
0 5 10 15
Kilometers

were made of steel and painted over with a thin coat of rubber to thinly disguise them as rubber bullets. Gergana, one of the architects working with me, with a Bulgarian mother and a Palestinian father, was smiling. She cheerfully told me that the bullets could be worn in a necklace: 'We make a hole and wear it. Shall I get the holes made for you?'

Visualizing Palestine as a landscape with economic potential requires a major shift in the trajectory of how this land has so far been imagined and represented by both communities. Its redemption as either the Holy Land or the idyllic Promised Land has no relevance to its future in the next century, nor is its place in the Arab dream as a land of gardens and tiled houses useful to the Palestinians. The potential of this landscape cannot be realized through pilgrimages and tourism to medieval and ancient sites. One needs to accept the landscape of the entire territory and its history as one idea to begin a dialogue on potential. Malcolm Wagstaff from the Geography Department of Southampton University has introduced relevant contemporary analysis and thought to the historical perspective of this region. Geography looks at territories and landscapes beyond the artificial political boundaries of recently born nation-states. The geography of the landscape and its utilization for accumulation and survival perforce views the region as a whole. Economic potential is therefore closely allied with geographical features.

> Since at least the work of their Palestinian colleague, Mukaddasi, active in the second half of the nineteenth century, geographers have recognized three or four parallel zones running north–south through the terrain of As, Sam, particularly Palestine. These are:
>
> 1. The Coastal Zone
> 2. The Central Uplands
> 3. The Valley of the Jordan River (the Ghor).

These three zones are the key to the future of Palestine and Israel. They link together the economic, physical and social dimensions of the land. The Crusaders had targeted holy places of

Some typical places that feature in Palestinian dreams about their lost land can still can be found: the rare olive-terrace cottages, for instance, which are disappearing fast as the Palestinian diaspora pours funds into mindless multi-storeyed concrete blocks that stand empty — waiting for the peace process to begin.

pilgrimage for occupation. The state of Israel is however an altogether different creature. With its sophisticated and educated military mind spearheading the occupation process, it has targeted each of these three zones separately and in a well-articulated campaign of sequential occupation. The formation of the archipelago of reservations on the West Bank seems to be part of its final campaign to integrate the central uplands into the main Israeli economy.

The period between 1948 and 1967 established their occupation of the fertile coastal zone. This zone consists of a plain which varies in width from five to forty kilometres. The soil on its surface has a variety that includes clay, gravel and sand. During those nineteen years the Palestinians were driven out or herded into Gaza, Akko, Jaffa or other confined camp ghettos. The war of 1948 established a corridor-link between the cities of the coastal zone and the central uplands, and provided guaranteed access to Jerusalem, which is situated in the mountains. These uplands, the land of Samaria and Judaea, consist of a series of mountain clusters which rise up to 900 metres above the surface of the Mediterranean. These are the lands which more or less define the imagined and negotiated territories of the Palestinian nation. While the land of

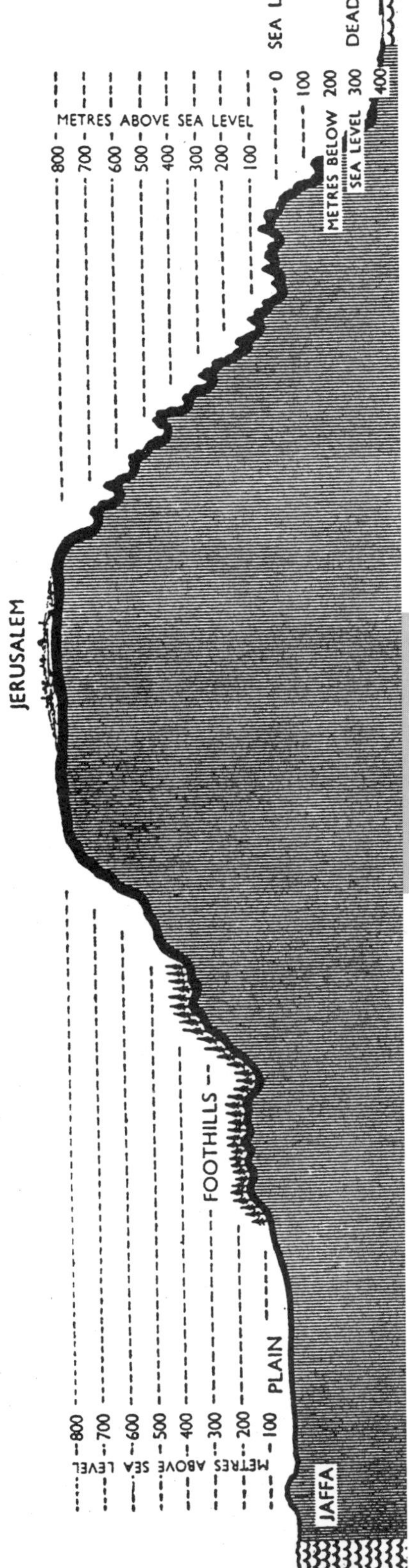

Cross-section through the land of Canaan showing the elevated location of Jerusalem and the three climatic zones.

Samaria is open and full of fertile valleys, the land of Judaea is essentially composed of limestone and rock.

The third zone of the Jordan valley is part of the Palestinian dream of a contiguous homeland with Jordan. Into this territory, the Israeli state has introduced a string of settlements. In a series of antagonistic strategic moves, the state has identified upland locations for settlement which effectively block any clear contiguous territorial flow from Palestine to Jordan. This desert rift valley, irrigated by the waters of the Jordan river as it runs below sea-level into the Dead Sea, is cordoned off with two barbed-wire fences which are patrolled by military jeeps round the clock.

While, as units of landscape, these three zones may have remained stable, their surface and underground exploitation by the Israeli military has transformed the region's irrigation and transportation, and urban and agrarian settlements in the coastal lowlands. Flat lands have been reclaimed and light sandy-soil lands have been organized into large units of efficiently run, capital-intensive farmlands. The farmlands have been connected to the irrigation system of the National Water Carrier which takes water from the Sea of Galilee to the Negev desert. The coastal zone functions as a single economic unit because of the large investments made in urbanization, transportation and irrigation.

In contrast, the central uplands have been devastated by physical, political and economic fragmentation. Before these highlands were originally subjected to human occupation, there is evidence to show that it was a wooded area. However, over the centuries, the wood from this region was exploited by every conqueror of the lowland. As the wood was carried away and used as fuel or for construction, replanting was forgotten. Somehow the occupiers were never able to invest in such long-term strategies as were needed to await the ripe old age that cedars need to become dense and hard. Today both Samaria and Judaea are relatively barren. The inevitable soil erosion that followed was countered by terracing the land with rough limestone walls. These terraces cover the hills of Palestine and are sadly neglected today as the

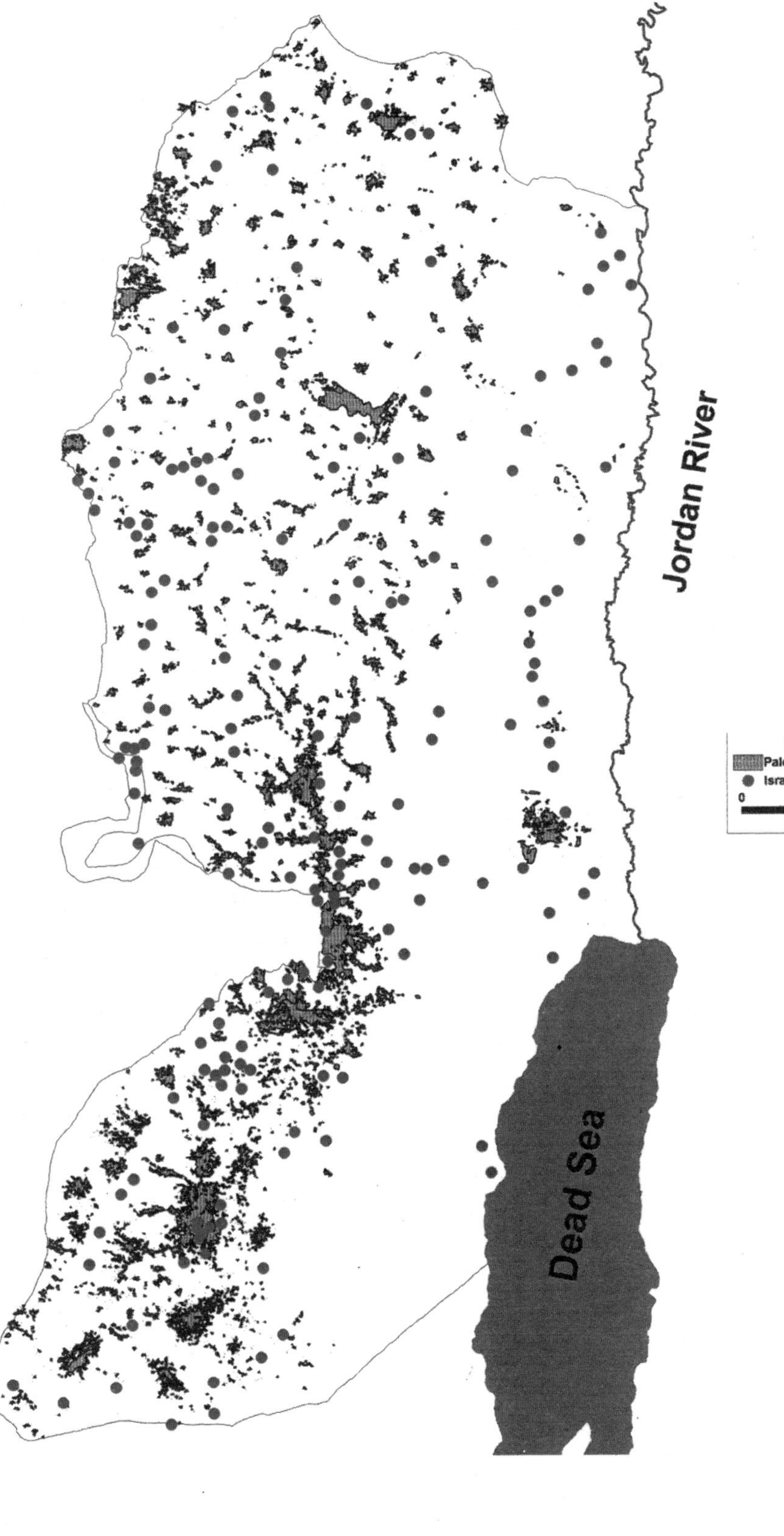

Map showing the location of Palestinian communities and Israeli settlements. The Israeli settlements (black dots) have been carefully planned along the Jordan river valley to interrupt any contiguous flow between Palestinian territory and Jordan.

agricultural economy of the area spirals downwards. Earlier, terracing had increased the productivity of the land and provided a livelihood for the numerous habitations that once dotted the region. Apart from providing a series of level surfaces for agriculture, these terraces trapped the run-off water from rainfall. This trapped water seeped into the ground and built up the aquifers that lie under the hills. Mountains are the natural regions where maximum precipitation takes place. In ancient times, before terracing diverted the water to the aquifers, the run-off used to reach the lowlands where it formed swamps. The territory defined as Palestine today sits on the major aquifer resource for Israel and Palestine. The aquifer is the state property of Israel. Flagstaff informs us that these terraces were built in the Bronze Age in a 'predetermined fashion with material brought from elsewhere and dumped behind stone walls'. The terracing system is fragile:

> . . . they are preserved only so long as certain conditions are fulfilled. These are, first, a population level above a certain critical threshold, for terraces require constant maintenance, second, farming methods of a traditional character in which mechanization is limited, and third, perhaps the continuity of a certain pattern of cropping involving dry-farmed cereals, vines and olives.

Settlement patterns and economic systems are closely linked. The patterns in all the three zones have undergone changes since the Bronze Age, in response to the political and economic changes that swept across these lands over the centuries. When we move away from the politicization of the archaeology of temples and forts, it is possible to view more dispassionately the evidence of archaeological finds in the rural landscape. The current settlement patterns in the coastal lowlands and in the uplands are part of the continuity of change that determines the economic prospects of this area. It is apparent that these settlement patterns continue to be mutually dependent and form part of a whole system in which all three zones form interdependent components. Each zone has its own special character and potential and no amount of territorial fragmentation into archipelagos can break its natural wholeness.

The coastal zone, for instance, has been a route for the movement of armies travelling between Egypt and the upper Levant and Europe. It was a route used by the Pharonic armies, Alexander and Napoleon. This zone has always been a land of insecurity and was consequently populated by nomads till as late as the nineteenth century. The attacks on the surveyors of the Holy Land sent out by the Palestine Exploration Fund confirmed the hazards of travelling along the coastline. By contrast, the village and urban settlements in the highlands were always relatively secure from such attacks. Flagstaff mentions that 'even in the late sixteenth century, 93 per cent of all registered nomadic communities in Palestine were located in the coastal zone'. Using Amiran's records of the Ottoman period, Flagstaff points out that at the end of the sixteenth century, 64 per cent of the settled communities were concentrated in the uplands and only 22 per cent in the coastal zone. Already the pattern had significantly changed from when many of the important urban settlements in the early Canaan period were located in the coastal zone, deriving investments from the Egyptian empire.

In the nineteenth century, the location of urban towns began to shift back to the coastal zone where the Canaanite civilization had at one time been located. Land was relatively underutilized in this area, and it attracted new settlers and provided the space for overflows from the mountain zone. Some of the early Jewish settlers began to migrate to Palestine in the later part of the century. The Ottoman land reforms had a significant effect on holding and ownership rights, which favoured individual titles and primogeniture inheritance. Collective management and mainten-ance of the elaborate system of hill-terracing had been much easier to galvanize in the pre-Ottoman period. Ottoman reform efforts made individual owners maintain only their own fields in working order. The process of Jewish settlement, which began in the 1880s, was boosted after 1948. Flagstaff quotes Falah: '95.5 per cent of the 81 "obliterated" Arab villages were in the plains.'

The lands of Samaria and Judaea.

The post-1948 pattern of exploitation of the coastal zone significantly altered the economy of the land of Palestine in at least two ways. Firstly, the occupation and exploitation of the coastlands and lowlands stabilized under Israeli management. The process of urbanization densified into suburbia in large lengths of the coastal edge. The Arab population in the coastal zone was encouraged to inhabit the remains of some of the villages they had lived in during the pre-1948 period. Two such villages that I visited had been 'conserved'. Akko, for one, still had its historical morphology although I could not but help sense the ghettoized isolation that was apparent when one considered the affluent housing developments that surrounded the place. Here the rights of ownership of Arab properties in perpetuity hangs in the balance. There is no assurance that houses can be passed on from father to son. The historic city walls are also the enclosing devices of an Arab culture that is encouraged to change its way of life. Akko has been conserved, preserved, bound and isolated. The advancing multi-storeyed housing developments have squeezed the Arabs to the tip of the coast.

The agricultural, industrial and transportation systems are part of the highly developed and relatively stable infrastructure of Israel. Since 1967, the Israeli settlements that have rained down on the uplands have transformed the landscape of Samaria and Judaea. In the post-1967 era, 'most of the 140 completely destroyed Arab villages are located in the Uplands'. The placement of heavily-armed settlements in the midst of a territory promised to the Palestinian people has overlaid the Palestinian landscape with agrarian and urban nodes which belong to an economy that is centred in the lowlands. In other words, the placement of these altogether alien economic nodes in the historical landscape of Palestine has effectively dislodged the historical, geographical and economic modes of production in the uplands. The economy of the region is proceeding in regression towards an apartheid economy that not only lays waste the land but also dehumanizes an entire population, which is one of the great resources of the area. This

Akko, on the north coast of Israel, has been conserved. Its Arab inhabitants, preserved, bounded and isolated, live in a cultural reservation.

Jaffa has been
converted from an
earlier affluent
Arab town into a
suburb of Tel Aviv,
and renamed Yafo.
Here, green lawns
stretch over the
ruins of
demolished Arab
houses and
provide the Arabs
with images of
how life can be
lived within an
Israeli reservation.
Is this the future
of the Palestinian
civilization?

pattern of establishing fortified, armed settlements on Palestinian lands seems to be intended to siphon off rather than mutually develop the region.

Apart from the land resource, which is forcibly occupied for settlements, water is taken from the aquifers and the natural rivers of occupied southern Lebanon (the Litani) and the Golan Heights of Syria (upper tributaries of the Jordan).

Israel and Palestine constitute a very small nation-state in the global overview of economies. Their entire population is less than half that of Bombay. And yet both get world attention that is entirely disproportionate to their insignificant size. Their land and economy is the subject of innumerable studies and publications. There are over twenty-five United Nations agencies located in Palestine. As for the economy of this region, there are many versions of and diagnoses for the Palestinian economy. Perhaps the World Bank summarizes the situation in the least alarmist manner:

> Structural imbalances and distortions resulting from heavy dependence on outside sources of employment for the occupied Palestinian territory, the unusually low degree of industrialization, a trade structure heavily dominated by trading links with Israel and with a large trading deficit and inadequacies in the provision of public infrastructure and services.

The Israeli army has devastated the economy of Palestine. To an observer like myself, the words of the Director of the Jerusalem Media and Communications Centre are much blunter – an expression of bluntness that the gentlemen of the World Bank can scarcely afford to admit in the formal pages of one of their documents. The Palestinian economy has been kept in a stranglehold

> . . . by a complex network of military orders that have the power of law in the occupied territories. These military orders cover and control all facets of economic activity in the Palestinian territories . . . with the objective of the occupier in manipulating and transforming the Palestinian territories . . . and the Palestinian economy into a

state of dependency, prolonging the occupation and thus forcing the Palestinians from their homeland. Israeli laws and policies have . . . tightened Israel's absolute control over water, restricting permits for industrial projects, creating a situation of unequal competition . . . forcing more than half the Palestinian work force to become cheap migrant labour working for the Israeli industrial and services sector.

Some 1,500 military laws, issued by Israeli army commanders, regulate economic life in Palestine. The Israeli area commander is endowed with all legislative, executive and judicial powers over Palestine. I propose to look at just one sector of the economy to illustrate the nature of the problems that need to be overcome to restore balance to the economies of Israel and Palestine. I hope to argue through this examination that Israel is destroying the character and potential of its own economy which, instead of being a balanced regional economy, has perforce become a parasitic and imbalanced one. In so arguing, I will move closer to my proposal whose central concern is restoration of balance in the economy and development of the potentials of the resources of both the Palestinians and the Israelis.

The land of Palestine is largely sandy and rocky. Water is crucial for sustaining a livelihood and is central to the accumulation of wealth. Three military orders issued for the West Bank have effectively captured the water resources of the Palestinians. They call it 'the great water robbery'. Military order 92 (1967) rescinds all existing laws relating to water which the Jordanians had earlier laid down. It appoints an Israeli official to appoint and control all water authorities on the West Bank. Military order 158 (1967) prohibits any water extraction or collection instrument to be installed without a permit. Any permit so issued can be revoked or amended at any time without assigning any reason. Military order 291 (1968) rescinds all and any earlier settlement of disputes amongst parties. It gives quasi-judicial powers to officers appointed by military order 92. In 1967, after winning the war, the Israeli military destroyed 140 Palestinian water-pumps in the Jordan valley and virtually closed down the Palestinian farms along the river valley. The urgent thirst

Staging Jewish settlements in the hills of Judaea and Samaria. First the bulldozers move in, then the porta cabins go up and the first batch of settlers begin to live in them. Gradually the developers arrive and the settlement becomes permanent. Images taken from three different locations.

for water in the Israeli economy has not yet stabilized. In 1949 Israel consumed less than 20 per cent of its renewable water resources. This increased to 95 per cent five years later. Within thirty years Israeli consumption of water exceeded the renewable supply. Water is the key to prosperity in the region, as is land. After fifty years and several wars and skirmishes, Israel has extended its control over the entire domain of the water resources of Palestine and Israel.

The geographical area within the national boundaries of Palestine and Israel is just over 27,000 square kilometres, of which 1,000 square kilometres cover water bodies. Palestine has 6,000 square kilometres and Israel has 20,000 square kilometres of territory. Thus, only just over a fifth of the area is under Palestine (Gaza and the West Bank). The total water supply for this area that is renewable is some 580 million cubic metres, of which rivers supply half. Almost a third comes from aquifers, the rest being run-off and brackish groundwater. Israel has, by comparison, a water supply of some 1,650 million cubic metres (three times), of which almost 60 per cent is from aquifers. Despite the obvious imbalance in the available water supply to the two communities, Israel takes over a quarter of its water requirement from aquifers under the West Bank, which constitutes almost 95 per cent of the West Bank's resource. In other words, Israel takes all the water supply from Palestinian sources and sells some of it back to the Palestinians for their needs.

The *Jerusalem Post* of 10 August 1990 carried a full-page advertisement issued by the Israeli Ministry of Agriculture on 'The Question of Water: Some Dry Facts'. It is a long detailing of justifications:

> This is an important point to ponder for those advocates of Israeli concessions who believe the Jews should have a viable independent state in their ancient homeland. It is important to realize that the claim to continued Israeli control over Judaea and Samaria is not based on extremist fanaticism or religious mysticism but on a rational, healthy and reasonable survival instinct.

The advertisement concludes thus:

> Finally, relinquishing control over Judaea and Samaria will leave Israel
> without any legal, moral or practical means to prevent the
> repatriation of almost a million Palestinians resident in refugee
> camps in surrounding Arab countries, whether by their own free will
> or by forcible 'transfer' by their reluctant Arab 'hosts'. Such a wave of
> poverty-stricken humanity would generate an impossible strain on
> the already over-extended water supply and inadequate sewage
> system, endangering further Israel's vulnerable and fragile source of
> life. It is difficult to conceive of any political solution consistent with
> Israel's survival that does not involve complete continued Israeli
> control of the water and sewage systems and of the associated
> infrastructure, including the power supply and road network,
> essential to their operation, maintenance and accessibility.

The economy of Palestine in Judaea and Samaria, like that of
any other semi-arid country, depends upon water. Thus, reliable use
of water for urban and agricultural economic production needs
security of water resources and sources by those who regulate the
economy. Water constraints have made Palestine deficient in food,
affecting the major crops of the West Bank — olives, fruits, grapes
and wheat.

The control of water by Israel is an extraordinary
phenomenon. It is so blatantly repressive that it is devoid of even
the most elementary semblance of humanitarianism. Fascinated by
this system of control, I began to look for the instruments of
control. One of the features of the archipelago of reservations
imposed on the Palestinians by the Oslo Accord is that water
cannot be exported from one area to another. The instrument of
control is the Mekorot Company, which is a monopoly Israeli water
supply company. Under Israeli law, Palestinian owners cannot tap or
use water without permits. All Palestinians have to receive their
water supply from Mekorot. In 1982, Mekorot acquired a lease on
the entire West Bank water for forty-nine years. Subsequent interim
agreements have provided some water rights to the Palestinians,

Al-Ouja near Jericho in 1990. Irrigated cultivation of Palestinian lands is becoming more difficult by the day as peace gets indefinitely postponed and Israel continues to regulate the water of Palestine.

but these remain insignificant. These concessions relate to specific bores into the aquifers and imposed water extraction quotas. A Palestinian applying for a licence to dig a well requires eighteen approvals, which include ministerial and Mekorot approvals. This process could take up to five or more years. Water in the Palestinian areas is militarily controlled. When, after 1967, Israeli troops fanned out to control the central uplands, five of the most important springs were surrounded by a barbed-wire fence which defined the area within as a 'National Reserve', and these were further enclosed within a 'military area'.

Inevitably, the conflict over water resources has resulted in a distortion of the economic prospects of the region. While Palestinians view the water regulations as a form of dispossession, the Israelis view it as a central issue in their ideology. Such use of an economic resource for ideological purposes has naturally distorted the economies of both communities. Over the last half a century of harvesting the water of the region, Israel has doubled the area of its irrigated land and trebled its consumption for industrial use. Conversely, the terraced fields of the West Bank mountains are being abandoned due to the non-viability of agriculture, the main reason being lack of water for irrigation. 35 per cent of the Palestinian economy is agriculture-based. In Israel the corresponding proportion is 3 per cent.

In order to diffuse this antagonism, it is necessary to work towards realizing the agricultural potential of the mountainous area, which is built over the major aquifers in the region. Water needs to be used for exploring the full productive potential of this region and needs to be transported across the territory from north to south to enable regeneration of this entire zone. It is therefore a crucial element in my proposal.

The aquifer is an economic resource that is being diverted away from its natural use as the most important factor of production in this semi-arid landscape. Its use for watering the extensive lawns and golf-courses of the coastal zone cannot be regarded as anything but antagonistic, particularly since over 80 per cent of the groundwater of Palestine is controlled by Mekorot.

Unfortunately, the issue of linking water resources to the economic potential of the land has been seldom discussed. Although the Oslo Accord set up a joint institutional framework under article 40, and a multilateral working group composed of Germans, Jordanians, Israelis and Palestinians, this group's discussion is confined to increasing the water resources through desalinization and transportation from outside the territory by sea and land pipes. Rational distribution of existing resources is left unexplored – beyond the brief of any working group.

In arguing for the economic sectors of Israel and Palestine to be integrated and made interdependent, my proposal has a specific thrust as a catalyst for radical economic transformation. It is disturbing that while the European Economic Community, the United States, the World Bank and other donors are pouring aid into the Balkans for 'structural reform' to help them out of the dismantled Soviet empire, none of the money that is being pledged to Palestine, which is ten times more in per capita terms, seems clearly marked for 'structural reform'. My proposal, therefore, is to be seen as part of a structural reform process for a country that needs radical surgery and not saline drips. If the Palestinian economy has been distorted by its imbalances and its lack of a hinterland and market, the Israeli economy too is imbalanced. Distortions have been caused in the Israeli economy by excessive exploitation of cheap labour from Palestine. In 1987, for example, 88 per cent of Israeli textile factories were dependent on labour from Gaza. Subsequent capitalization and automation has reduced this figure. The Labour Ministry's Manpower Planning Authority has candidly admitted: 'If the Palestinian workers were to suddenly disappear overnight, the Israeli economy would find itself in chaos.' Deeper damage to the economy of the region has however been caused by the impoverishment of the upland zone of the West Bank. Although the zone is integral to the economic potential of the region, it has been amputated from the main body-economic. The metropolitan-led economy of Israel has grown at the expense of its

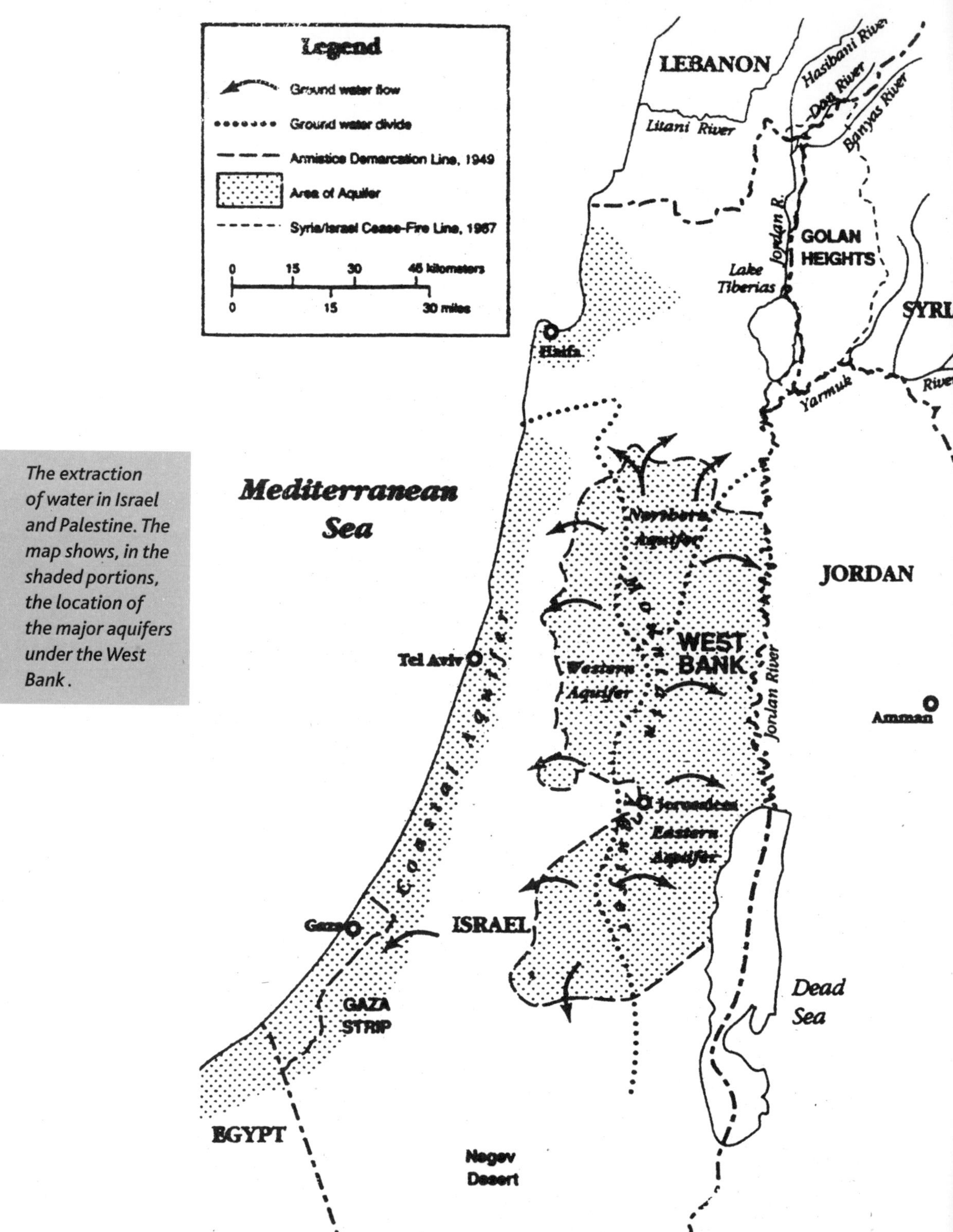

The extraction of water in Israel and Palestine. The map shows, in the shaded portions, the location of the major aquifers under the West Bank.

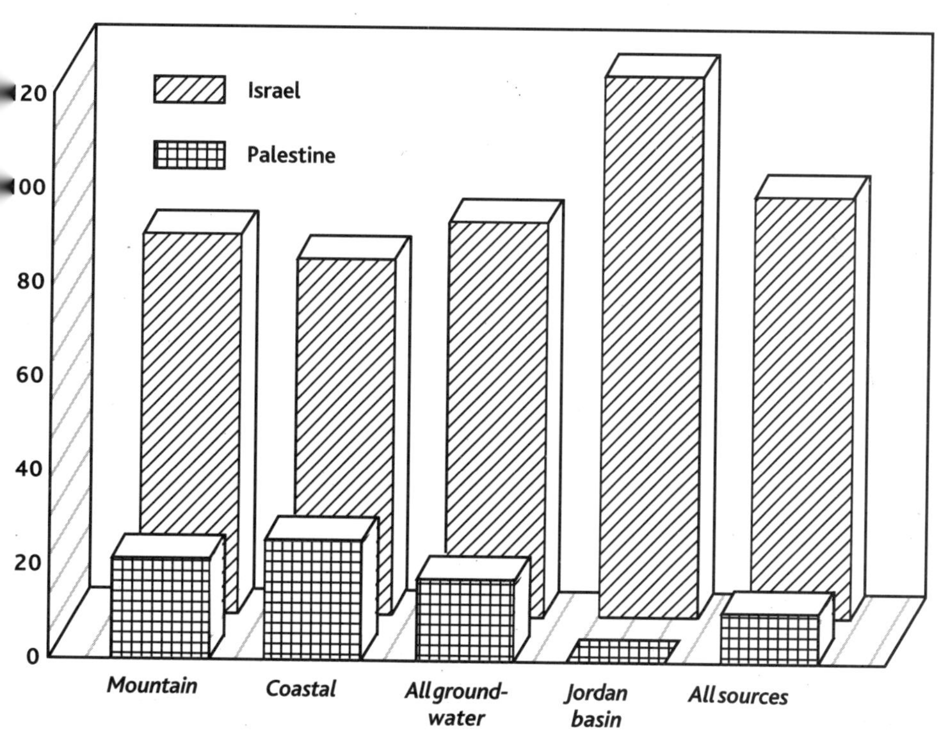

Graph showing the pattern of water consumption of Israel and Palestine.

neighbourhood, funded by the generously-donated efforts of the international Jewish community. Further holocaust compensations will extend this distortion. Israel's mortal fear of the dormant competitive abilities of the Palestinians has to be seen as a manifestation of the fear of a prey surrounded by alien Arab economies. Its social, political and economic isolation certainly fuels this fear which is defended by aggressive stances. Lebanon, Iraq, Jordan, Saudi Arabia, Syria and Egypt have not yet formed an economic union. But if they do so and extend this to a military union, the prospects for Israel's dreams of living in peace seem somewhat on the edge of a nightmare. The political geography of Israel places a grossly underdeveloped and distorted Palestinian economy in its centre. The rich perfumed economy of Israel is surrounded by thorns in the form of economies in the midst of the political and social instabilities of underdevelopment. The Israeli military sees borders as frontiers and neighbours as enemies. They are not paid or trained to imagine ways to extend the future economic potential of this region as a whole. For them, the three geographical zones are not integrated parts of a single economy with different character and potential but a series of frontiers to be defended with fortifications.

The population of Israel has been increased by massive emigration to almost twice that of Palestine. Russian is the second language on the streets. Its economy, however, is twenty-four times larger than the Palestinian one, which keeps spinning in perpetual recession. There is not much difference between the price-levels of commodities in the markets of Palestine and Israel. Yet, Israeli per capita national income is some seven times larger than that of Palestine. All of this is documented in the volumes of reports that donor agencies prepare before they identify projects for funding. Just about every United Nations agency dealing with social issues and development is represented either in Gaza or the West Bank. Millions of dollars are promised. Some of the funds get transferred to Palestinian ministries. Consultants prepare reports that are intended to run projects to support Palestinian efforts at achieving statehood. But investment in the Palestinian economy is avoided by anyone looking for returns. Palestine is bad news. At the 1996 World Bank Consultative Group meeting held in Paris, a pledge was made of $881 million. Between 1996 and 1998 the Palestinian per capita income fell by 24 per cent. Families survive by pooling incomes together. The average size of a family is seven persons, as the Israelis keep reminding the world. There is no money for recreation, parks are crowded with picnickers at weekends, and cafeterias usually serve one coffee to long-sitting customers. The roadside *falafel* stalls do roaring business and the restaurants in Ramallah are as expensive as those in Jaffa Street in West Jerusalem. The donor pledges for 1994–95 by the European Union, Japan, the United States, United Nations and the World Bank was $1500 billion. So far less than one billion of the donors' money has been dispersed in Palestine. 'They have problems in digesting the funds', I was told.

The reports on the economic and social conditions in the West Bank and Gaza Strip read like epitaphs of a nation that is yet to be born. Palestine is completely dependent on Israel. It imports over 90 per cent of its requirements from Israel. Palestine has a trade deficit of just under a billion dollars, of which a tenth is due to insufficiency of food. The Israeli military is slowly strangling the Palestine economy. By controlling the use of water in the West Bank they have engineered a depopulation of villages, which are surrounded by abandoned terraces. In 1980, 76 per cent of the migrants in the West Bank were from villages. All of this labour has entered the growing pool of the unemployed on the streets of the towns of the West Bank. From this pool, Israel is able to engage and dismiss workers at will. United Nations data inform us that over one-sixth of the West Bank's labour force seek employment in Israel. The Palestinians estimate this figure to be 36 per cent. Periodically, the military imposes the dreaded 'closures' – military refusals at checkpoints to let labour into Israel. These closures reduce the wage-earnings to two-thirds of what they ought to be during normal attendance.

FRANCE
AUSTRIA
HUNGARY
SWITZ
Nantes
Basel
Wien
München
Bordeaux
Genève
Lyon
Milano
Torino
Po
Genova
Nice
MONACO
Ljubljana
Zagreb
Beograd
YUGOSLAVIA
Split
Toulouse
Marseille
ANDORRA
La Coruña
Bilbao
Porto
Valladolid
SPAIN
Madrid
PORTUGAL
Valencia
Barcelona
Ajaccio
Corsica
Roma
ITALY
Napoli
Bari
Taranto
Tirana
ALBANIA
Lisboa
Sardinia
Cagliari
Mediterranean Sea
Palermo
Sicily
Catania
Ionian Sea
Cadiz
Gibraltar
Oran
Alger
Annaba
Binzert
Tunis
MALTA
Madeira (Port.)
Funchal
Tangier
Tetuan
Sidi-bel-Abbès
Constantine
Sfax
Rabat
Faz
Oujda
TUNISIA
Casablanca
Meknes
MOROCCO
Atlas Mountains
Tripoli
Al
Banghazi
Marrakech
Agadir
Gt. Western Erg
Gt. Eastern Erg
Canary Is. (Sp.)
Santa Cruz de Tenerife
ALGERIA
LIBYA
Las Palmas
El Aaiun
WESTERN
SAHARA
Dakhla
Tropic of Can
Tamanrasset
Mt. Tahat
3002
S A H A R A   D E S E
Nouadhibou
Emi Koussi
3415
MAURITANIA
Nouakchott
CAPE VERDE IS.
M A L I
Timbuktu
Agadez
NIGER
CHAD
Praia
Dakar
SENEGAL
Niger
Niamey
Lake
Chad
Abéché
Banjul
THE GAMBIA
Bamako
UPPER
VOLTA
Sokoto
Kano
Maiduguri
N'djamena
Bissau
Mt. Tamgue
Ouagadougou
GUINEA-BISSAU
Kaduna
Bauchi
GUINEA
Conakry
Freetowne
SIERRA
LEONE
IVORY
COAST
GHANA
Tamale
L. Volta
TOGO
BENIN
NIGERIA
Ibadan
Lagos
Benin City
Pt. Harcourt
Sarh
Galoua
Benue
Monrovia
LIBERIA
Kumasi
Abidjan
Accra
Lome
Cotonou
Sekondi-
Takoradi
Douala
Bioko
CAMEROUN
Bangui
AFRICA
Yaounde
Berberati
Kaduna

MOLDAVIAN
Krivol Rog
Zaporozh'ye
Rostov-na-Donu
Volga
Gur'yev
KAZAKH S.S.R.
Aral'sk
Odessa
Crimea
Krasnodar
Stavropol'
Astrakhan'
Aral Sea
Kyzl-Orda
Muyu
Kum
Bucuresti
Simferopol'
Novorossiysk
Armavir
Kyzyl-Kum
Dzha
Varna
Black Sea
Sochi
Caucasus Mts
Groznyy
Ordzhonikidze
Nukus
Chimkent
Tashkent
Istanbul
Bosporus
Sinop
GEORGIA
Batumi
Tbilisi
ARMENIA
Kirovabad
Baku
Krasnovodsk
Kara-Kum
TURKMEN S.S.R.
UZBEK S.S.R.
Bukhara
Samarkand
Ankara
Trabzon
Leninakan
Yerevan
AZERBAYDZHAN
Caspian Sea
Ashkhabad
TADZH
Dushanbe
Bursa
Eskisehir
TURKEY
Kayseri
L. Van
Tigris
Urmia
Tabriz
Kopeh Dagh
Mazar-i-Sharif
Faizaba
Izmir
Konya
Antalya
Adana
Gaziantep
KURDISTAN
Rasht
Damavand
Mashhad
Herat
Kabul
Hin
Aleppo
Euphrates
Mosul
Tehran
AFGHANISTAN
Peshaw
Levkosia
(Nicosia)
Larnaca
SYRIA
Homs
Kirkuk
Hamadan
Qom
Dasht-i-Kavir
IRAN
CYPRUS
Beirut
LEBANON
Damascus
Baghdad
Kermanshah
Farah
Kandahar
Ra
Shah Faisa
Tel Aviv
PALESTINE
Jerusalem
Amman
JORDAN
Syrian
Desert
IRAQ
Najaf
Esfahan
Ahvaz
Basra
Abadan
Quetta
Multi
PAKIST
Alexandria
Port Said
Suez
Cairo
Giza
Faiyum
SINAI
Gulf of Aqaba
Nafud
KUWAIT
Kuwait
Shiraz
BALUCHISTAN
Nile
Asyut
Gulf of Suez
Bandar 'Abbas
Indus
S
EGYPT
Luxor
Red
SAUDI
Dhahran
Hufhuf
BAHRAIN
QATAR
Doha
The Gulf
Ras al Khaimah
Dubai
Abu Dhabi
Gulf of Oman
Hyderabad
Karachi
SIND
HEJAZ
Medina
NEJD
Riyadh
UNITED ARAB
EMIRATES
Muscat
Ahm
Aswan
Lake
Nasser
Sea
Jeddah
Mecca
ARABIA
Ra
Wadi Halfa
Port Sudan
Rub' al Khali
OMAN
Arabian
Nile
Atbarah
ERITREA
YEMEN
Hadramawt
Bom
Omdurman
Khartoum
Asmara
Hodeida
YEMEN
San'a'
P.D.R.
Mukalla
Sea
SUDAN
Sennar
El Obeid
Ta'izz
Aseb
Aden
Gulf of Aden
Socotra
(Yemen P.D.R.)
arra
Sudd
White Nile
Blue Nile
Ras Dashan
4620
L. Tana
DJIBOUTI
Djibouti
Cape Guardafui
Malakal
ETHIOPIA
Berbera
Wau
Addis Ababa
SOMALI REPUBLIC
Juba
L.
Turkana

The dehumanization of employed Palestinian workers is not limited to closures. A fifth of each wage-earner's pay packet is taken back by Israeli employers and put into the Keren Hanikuyim Fund. Workers from Gaza contribute some $36 million a year to this fund, out of which monies go towards the public expenditure and civil administration of the state of Israel. The International Labour Organization was unable to get details of this fund from the Ministry of Defence. Gideon Eshet wrote in 1991, in the *Yediot Aharanot*: 'Hard it is to believe, if you are not a settler or a soldier, and just an Arab who lives in the West Bank, you are taxed more than a person in Israel with the same income. We asked the Civil Administration why – and were told: "That's how it is".'

In 1980 the total labour force in Palestine was 308,000. When I was working on projections for the demand for schools in the future I was surprised to see the 1997 population statistics. The bars of the graph for ages up to four years is the large base of the population pyramid. It will place an enormous number of people in the labour market in fifteen years. The graph is disturbing because if the agricultural land of the West Bank has been forcibly dried up, current Israeli policies will ensure that the working population of Palestine will be reduced to degraded poverty in another decade.

Jerusalem and Its Trenches

If you walk out through the recently-punched openings of the western walls of Jerusalem at the Dung Gate, you can explore its early history. A descending path leads you into Kidron Valley, the valley of hell, 'Jahannam', to the Arabs and Satan's river to the Christians. Isam Awwad Islam explained to me, as we walked into the Dome of the Rock:

> On the Day of Judgement there will be a fine chord stretched between the Dome of the Rock and the Mount of the Olives. Those souls who can cross over on this chord, will reach Paradise on the Mount. Those that slip and fall will perish in Jahannam – Hell.

Awwad has the awesome responsibility of maintaining the

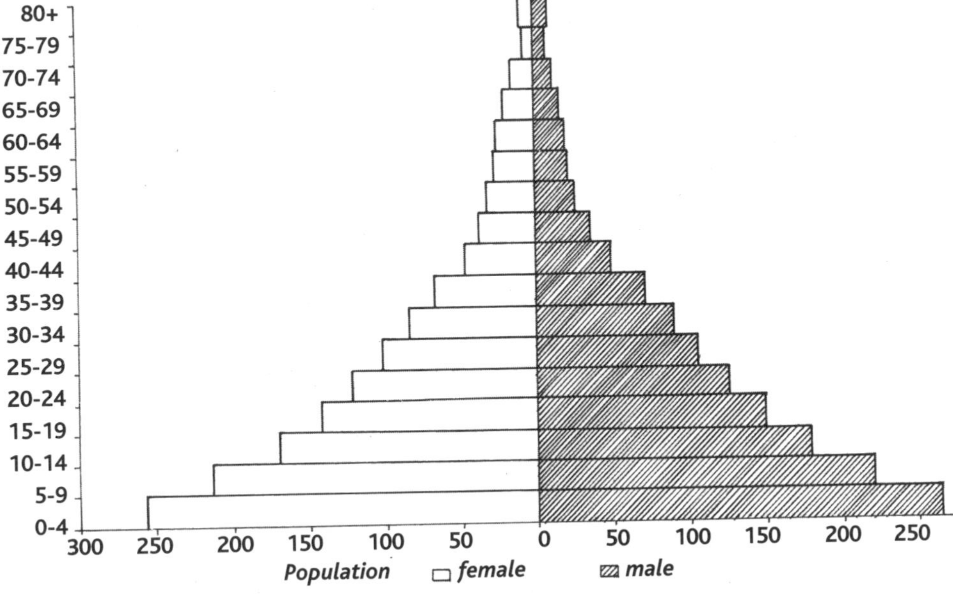

Above:
The 1997 population pyramid showing the large population that will enter the labour force in another fifteen years.
Below:
Palestinian workers wait for work at the Erez Checkpoint in Gaza.

entire Haram Sharif. He supervised the restoration of the dome of the Al-Aqsa mosque after an Australian tourist, Denis Michael Rohan, set it ablaze in 1969. Rohan had laughed and photographed the mosque as it burned.

When Michelangelo represented the Last Judgement in the Sistine Chapel, he showed some souls being rescued from the River of Satan as they had fallen off the chord by mistake. His representation of the satanic agent swatting the condemned souls with his oar remains etched in my memory. The image surfaced immediately as I walked to the bottom of the valley, below the Jewish graveyard on the right and the Muslim graveyard on the left. Apparently this is one of the most expensive burial-grounds in the city because, on the Day of Judgement, the souls of those already waiting in the Kidron Valley will be far ahead in the queue.

Kicking up dust next to the sewage drain that is being constructed in the valley, I arrived at the site of the City of David. Was it really the City of David? At every effort to delve into the history of Jerusalem one is confronted by an uncomfortable doubt – that ancient Jerusalem, or for that matter ancient Palestine or Israel, has been invented to synchronize with the needs of contemporary models that justify claims to the landscape and its power places. Jerusalem is the last and the first city of the Jews and hence is regarded by them as a higher level of claim than the claim of a third position in the Muslim hierarchy of sacred cities. The claims on both sides are intense, imagined and illusionary, because the Christians are inevitably left out of the antagonisms that are hurled. The state of Israel needs to support its tenuous claims over the contemporary old city. So Jerusalem is portrayed as an object or lost sacred relic in the memory and imagination of the Jews. The Palestinians' claim to Jerusalem is based on population statistics as well as its crucial role in the liturgy of Islam. 92 per cent of the inhabitants of old Jerusalem are said to be Arabs – Christians and Muslims.

Four trenches were.dug to search for the City of David between 1913 and 1982. Raymond Weil dug in 1913–14, J.W. Crowfoot in 1927–28, Kathleen Kenyon in 1961–67 and Yigal Shiloh in 1978–82. Despite all these searches in the haystack of history, Margaret Steiner comments that no architecture from the Late Bronze Age (1500–1200 BC) has been found. No evidence has been discovered that links the archaeological remains of the stone walls to David's City or to his occupation of this place. There have been no Arab digs in this area. They are not permitted. But the establishment of facts which prove David's presence in the city is important to the Jews. The Jewish claim on Jerusalem rests on the premise that David founded Jerusalem as the first Jewish city. The biblical narrative therefore has to supersede archaeological evidence. Archaeologists agree that there was a city in existence on these lower slopes below Salladin's wall, and the Old Testament informs us that David captured the city from the Jebusites who were an offshoot of the Canaanites. The available archaeological evidence fails to make any links between David and Jerusalem, or for that matter between Solomon and the First Temple in Jerusalem. But the basis of the Israeli claim to Jerusalem is that it was the site of their first royal city and their First Temple. The problems of historiography seem insurmountable. The absence of historical accounts which deal with ancient Palestine perforce makes us rely on biblical texts, which become disproportionately important because a historic narrative has to be forged to prop up contemporary claims to the city. The Hebrew bible designates many Late Bronze Age and Early Iron Age sites as 'Israeli sites'. The ethnic label presumes that these sites had specific identifiable Israeli remains as distinct from Canaanite remains. This shift is not endorsed by findings at the digs. Archaeology, as we have already seen, is something of an inconvenience for the state of Israel and for Jews in general. Since there has been no physical or historiographic evidence to support the biblical narrative of the Exodus or the United Kingdom, the claim in the Hebrew records needs correctly to be classified as 'suspended belief'. Unfortunately, such reconstructions of ethnic history preclude the possibility of considering the history of this region dispassionately as a history of the Levant in the same way as the current function of the Israeli

Kidron Valley, associated with the flowing rivers of hell, and its banks, the final resting-place for souls before the Day of Judgement. A precious grave-site for the Jewish. Inset: Scene from Michelangelo's Last Judgement in the Sistine Chapel showing souls being collected by Satanic messengers as they slip and fall into the valley of hell.

economy precludes the possibility of considering the economy of the Levant territory as one economy. Jerusalem too has been removed from its Levantine context and its future is proposed either as an Arab or an Israeli city.

The archaeology of Jerusalem can be divided into three parts – the biblical remains of David's fortifications, the historical nucleus of the inhabited city, the site on the hill contentiously referred to as Haram al Sharif or the Temple Mount. The last of these is the most problematic and volatile as disputed territory. The Haram al Sharif, the Arabs claim, is three times holy to Muslims throughout the world. Firstly, it was the Qibla originally before Mecca was proclaimed as the premier site. Secondly, the Prophet ascended to heaven from Jerusalem 'to within two bow-lengths of God' after travelling there from Mecca on his magical steed. Thirdly, Jerusalem is connected to life beyond the grave as it is the site at which, on the Day of Resurrection, the Last Judgement will take place. The Temple Mount, the same spot where Muslims gather in hundreds to pray every Friday, is thrice sacred to the Jews. It was the site of the first two temples; the place on the rock where Abraham prepared his son for sacrifice; and, most importantly, it is where the Third Temple is due to be built, to receive the coming Messiah.

In the last 1,900 years, Amos Elon tells us about Jerusalem,

> the dominant religion was changed at least eleven times, often at great human cost by the Romans in AD 70 and 132, the Byzantines in 335, the Zoroastrians in 614, the Byzantines in 628, the Arabs in 638, the Crusaders in 1099, the Arabs again in 1187, the British in 1917, the Jordanians in 1948 and the Israelis in 1967.

A special institute exists in Jerusalem to propagate the idea of undertaking the project for the Third Temple. Its shop is full of images of the ancient future that awaits Israel for delivering the Jews to paradise. It needs only an Arab holocaust to realize this dream. We are at the beginning of the twenty-first century and yet the orthodox Jews believe that reminders of exiles, exoduses and holocausts are needed to forge a Jewish identity. As a fool on the

Above:
The Haram Sharif.
The present future
of a Palestinian
Jerusalem.
Below:
On the same site,
the coming Third
Temple proposed
by temple groups
in Israel. This is
the ancient future
of an Israeli
Jerusalem.

hill, one cannot but smile. When crazed fanatics of the Hindu nationalist party in India demolished the Babri mosque, which had been in use till 1948, they believed that they would find the foundations of a mythical Hindu temple under it. The old bricks that lay scattered there probably belonged to a Buddhist *stupa*. That single act of demolition had enormous repercussions. It generated new antagonisms that will take decades to pacify. A tragedy of enormous human and social dimensions had been enacted. The Babri mosque had been used for prayers for centuries. The Haram al Sharif is the third most holy shrine to Muslims throughout the world. My proposal therefore does not attempt to resolve the fictitious self-invented problems of religious fundamentalists for the hill in Jerusalem. It focuses instead on the secular potential of the city, its economic potential and a distinct future removed from the restrictions of the past. In some ways, the proposal puts forward the idea that such a potential can only be realized if the scale and character of the space that is required as the site is so large and exciting that it considerably diminishes the collective impact of all the religious spaces in the city.

Above:
Jerusalem in 1935.
Below:
The city in 1995.

The Proposal, United Canaan

This proposal is an intervention into the current political, social economical and architectural situation in Palestine and Israel. At the political level it proposes that this part of the Ancient Levant, which has been variously called Palestine or Israel in this century, should be called Canaan in the next century. Its citizens are Canaanites and dwell in the two separate states of Palestine and Israel. Canaan is the United States or Federation of Palestine and Israel, with one national capital, Jerusalem, and two separate state capitals, Ramallah and Tel Aviv. This political proposal is not my invention obviously, but it does define the wider context for implementing the proposal. Incidentally, this has been the declared position of the Indian government for many years, for lasting peace in this land – one nation, two states.

At the social and economic level, the proposal advocates social separation and economic integration. It advocates development of the character and potential of each community and its contribution to the integrated economic activity of United Canaan, which is seen as a single economic territory. The question of Jordan being part of Canaan is left open, although it is my view that it needs to be integrated into the United Canaan economic system.

The architectural intervention consists of the opening up of a fast, new, highly sophisticated train that links the port of Haifa on the Mediterranean Sea to Tiberias on the Sea of Galilee in a crescent track via Nazareth. From Nazareth the train moves south, linking key Palestinian towns into a single market. It proceeds to Jenin, Nablus, Jerusalem, Bethlehem, Hebron and Beer Sheba. Here it turns east and ends its tracks at Gaza.

It is a train for the commuters of Canaan, for the goods of Canaan and, equally significantly, it is also a new national water-carrier that will bring water from the desalination plants of Haifa, the Sea of Galilee and the aquifers of the West Bank and distribute them to the starved agricultural terraces of the West Bank and the deserts of Negev. Both the train-track and the water-carrier are integrated. The carriages ride the water-carrying tube. Each station on this track is a new secular space that will be created to encourage new economic, social and political activities. The stations are concourses in which spaces ebb and flow in time – daytime, month time and annual time. They are the new realms of the mesocosmic activities that are deeply a part of the Arab sensibility. One such station is described here. It is situated in Jerusalem, outside Damascus Gate. Its architectural expression is indicative of how these concourses would work.

Maps, diagrams and images with the text describe the proposal in the following pages. These descriptions form the conceptual framework on which the architectural flesh has been outlined here as well as in the last chapter. This outline proposal has two interrelated components – Connectivity and Architecture.

Proposed *train travelling through a United Canaan landscape.*

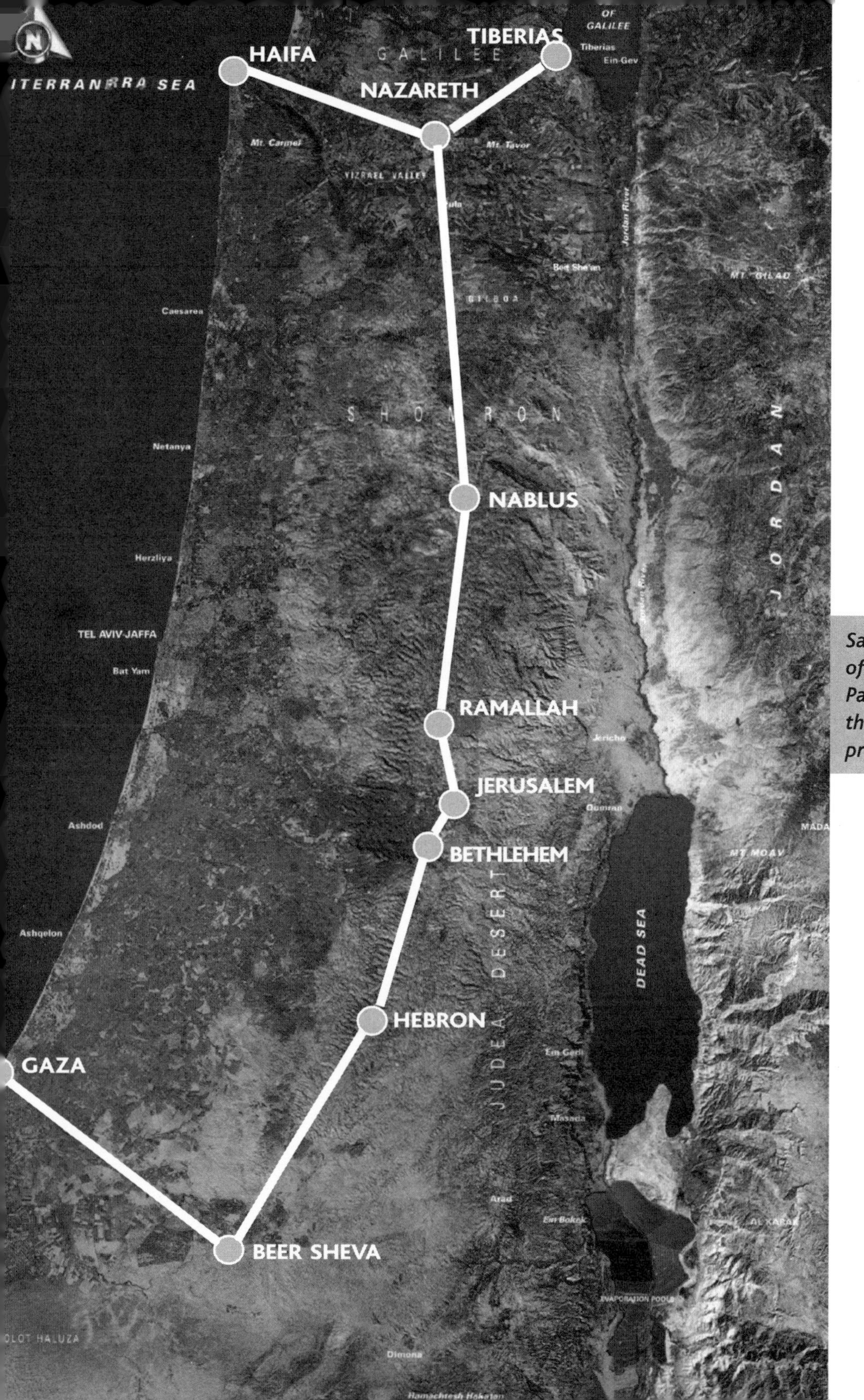

Satellite image of Israel and Palestine showing the route of the proposed train.

Connectivity through Transport and Water Resources

The existing road network in the land which will become United Canaan has been laid to isolate the Palestinians from the Israelis. The roads that connect the urban towns and villages in Israel are virtually closed to Palestinians, who may travel on them at risk of interrogation. The roads that connect the Palestinian urban towns and villages circumvent the Israeli roads or pass through fortified checkpoints of the Israeli army. A third category of the existing road network links Israeli settlements which have mushroomed on the West Bank. These are open only to Israelis. A yellow number-plate gets you the right to use all the road networks. A green numberplate confines you to the road network that connects Palestinian towns. A Palestinian in Jerusalem can have a yellow numberplate. Three kilometres away, in Ramallah, he can have only a green numberplate.

The proposed train moves across these ridiculous barriers. A new connectivity links all the important urban towns of the West Bank to towns in Israel. Old roads become disused. Two parallel movement systems cross United Canaan from north to south. The first, which travels along the coastlands, is already well developed. The second is the proposed intervention: it will travel along the uplands connecting communities and economies and integrating them into the new national infrastructure.

Water Resources

The track of the train is an integrated water and carriage-carrier. While the carriages connect the economy of manpower and produce, the water-carrier connects and irrigates the wasting lands of the West Bank. The water in the carrier is drawn from three sources – the new desalination plants yet to be placed in Haifa, the Sea of Galilee and the aquifers. This new water-carrier will enable a balancing of the consumption of water in United Canaan.

Architectural Component of the Proposal

William A. Rome Jr, writing in the *New York Times* of 3 March 1999, says:

> The drought this winter could be a portent of an even drier future unless Israel, Jordan and the Palestinians work together to conserve shared water resources, an international panel of scientists warned Tuesday.
>
> With a population of 12 million in a region with as much rainfall as Phoenix Arizona, water supplies 'are barely sufficient to maintain a quality standard of living', said Gilbert F. White, a geographer from the University of Colorado who was chairman of a research group from the US National Academy of Sciences and counterpart institutions from Israel, Jordan and the Palestinian Authority,
>
> Ancient underground aquifers are being drained dry, while scarce rains flow unused into desert gulches and rivers are diverted for water-intensive tropical agriculture, the researchers said. Watersheds cross political boundaries and can only be managed jointly, they said. Left carefully unmentioned were the consequences of a regional battle over dwindling water resources.

The water crisis has already been explained earlier and this newspaper report is quoted here to illustrate the need for joint management.

A number of spatial planning exercises for Jerusalem have already been encapsulated in definitive published volumes. Our present efforts must therefore be seen as part of a sequence of published statements by planners for a new Jerusalem. The old Jerusalem belongs to the Arabs. The new Jerusalem belongs to Israel. Between the two Jerusalems lies a fuzzy space – a buffer-zone – in which both communities fear to implement any radical changes. If they did, it would start a riot because it would shift the imagined lines of control and give advantage to one or the other of the two contenders. The Ottoman city walls neatly define old Jerusalem's boundaries. New Jerusalem is well settled around a city-centre full of boutiques and endless suburbia which are being created to try and balance the population statistics, so that the Jewish population appears in the census as the major population. As the municipal boundaries keep shifting to include more and more new Israeli settlements, the buffer-zone lies suspended in space, a transit-zone suspended in time.

During the British mandate Henry Kendall, an enthusiastic city

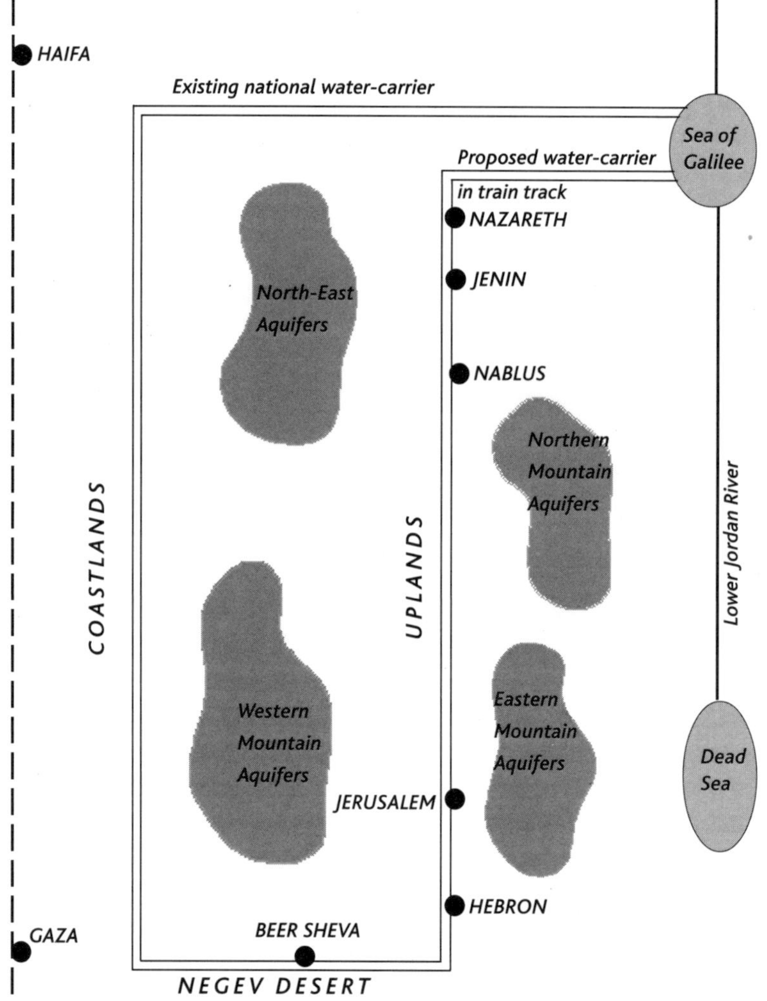

Schematic proposal of water resource connectivity in New Canaan. The proposed water-carrier travelling through Palestine and Israel coincides with the train route, and revives the strangled agriculture of the West Bank and the deserts of Israel.

engineer in charge of Jerusalem, published his City Plan. Issued by HMSO, this large volume, *Jerusalem City Plan, Preservation and Development during the British Mandate 1948*, contains all the data that planners consider necessary to appropriate space for city growth. There are comparative drawings of the growth of Jerusalem from 1918 onwards, and of green areas and commercial zones and all the densities and activities that made sense three decades ago as the basics of planning ideology.

Later, a series of master plans were proposed. In 1973 Ariel Sharon published his volume – *Jerusalem Planning: The City and Its Environs* (Weidenfeld and Nicholson). Sharon had earlier published the book *Physical Planning in Israel*, the textual and graphic work for which was carried out in 1951. I could not find the word 'Arab' in this volume. In 1986 Moshe Safdie published, through MIT Press, *The Harvard Jerusalem Studio: Urban Designs for the Holy City*. In all these influential works, efforts at physical planning dominated the proposals. In all these proposals it was implicitly indicated that the Arabs would do well to move to areas with boulevards and parks instead of living in a dense urban environment.

My proposal, however, is not just about spatial planning. To me, Jerusalem is not exclusively important for the prosperity of United Canaan; it is but a link in the chain. Jerusalem needs to be a mop that absorbs the aggressive energies of two civilizations that are bent on clashing with each other. On the ground, the Arab Christians and Muslims, and the Israelis and the Latin Christians compete for space. The mop is the station concourse. Its users are meso-Arabs, Jews, Orthodox and Latin Christians. The mesocity is the intermediate world between the macrocity and the microcity. The macrocity is the state and all its plans for the people who form the microcity. Physical planning processes bring the written laws and regulations of the state to the front door of the citizens and tend to regulate by planning all aspects of the citizen's life and behaviour outside his front door. If the macroprocess is the planned written process, the mesoprocess is the autonomous oral process.

The mesocity is the realm in which community relationships

Damascus Gate, leading into the heart of old Jerusalem — part of the Arab mesocity.

and public life are reciprocated by the private worlds of the members of the community. The mesocity is the repository of the deep oral culture of a community. Its inhabitants act in a city and do not try to know it. They talk about a city, they do not write about it. The space of a mesocity is a space that is inhabited by people of diverse cultural origins, who have been brought together into a synergetic relationship that depends on mutual integration without homogenization and without the obsession for so-called origins to define identities. These are spaces where the rubbing of polycultures initiates new creative activities, where the distinction between that which is modern and that which is traditional is difficult to make out, and where the regulations of the macroauthority lie suspended and redundant.

Mesocity space is not an extension of the written orders and spatial patterns of the city. It is a space dominated by the personal use of the community – it is a space where multiple operators reciprocate outside the macrosystem.

Robert Redfield and Milton Singer, in their paper, 'The Cultural Role of the Cities', perhaps best describe the qualities of a mesocity:

> One or both of the following things are true: (1) the prevailing relationships of people and the prevailing common understanding have to do with the technical not the moral order, with the administrative regulations, business and technical convenience; (2) these cities are populated by people of diverse cultural origins removed from the indigenous seats of their cultures. They are cities in which new states of mind, following from these characteristics, are developed and become prominent. The new states of mind are indifferent to or inconsistent with, or supersede or overcome, states of mind associated with local cultures and ancient civilization. The individuals of these . . . cities, if any, are intelligentsia rather than literati.

Contrary to this definition, new Jerusalem and the series of planning exercises that have tried to give a new future to Jerusalem have tried to convert Jerusalem into a city of literati 'which carry forward, develop, elaborate a long established local culture or civilization. These are cities that convert folk culture into its civilized dimensions and . . . moral order.'

Mesocity space carries the evolution of local cultures into the contemporary world without fear of the modern. Mesocity space keeps equidistant from religious and municipal dictates.

Macrocity space bulldozes and codifies local culture and replaces it with a written macromoral order.

The station concourse is a mesocosmic space. It carries forward local cultures; it enhances character and potential; it absorbs the antagonisms of macromoral orders. It accepts only the technical order of the space enclosure and the train. Within this it swirls, motivated by the inevitable integration of interdependent communities, each with its unique commercial and cosmic concerns. It is the space of oral cultures and their unlimited ability to continuously adjust to contemporary times according to their own needs.

The triangular site outside Damascus Gate is in the buffer-zone between the Israeli city of new Jerusalem and the Arab city of old Jerusalem. The Israeli city is a macrocity of written cultures. Here the moral order of Zion has been codified into a series of rules and regulations that preclude the possibility of emergent, everchanging moral orders which evolve out of the collaborations and negotiations of citizens interacting with and adjusting to their mutual needs. The Arab city, on the other hand, is a mesocity of intellectuals, of an oral culture that will not codify the moral order of its citizens into written rules and regulations. Here the community meshes its activities not along functional forms but on the basis of permissiveness, tolerance and a level of mutual adjustment that is of a high order.

The proposal creates within this site a large covered space into which the mesocity activities of the old city as well as from other cities can flow and develop. The train-line, its platforms and its intercity connections provide the technical order of the space with the bus station. The concourse, at minus 9-metre level, is the space in which the mesocity swirls with activity, whose moral, social and ethical order is governed by its inhabitants. Exits are provided on both sides of the rail-line. The platform to the west connects to the new Israeli Jerusalem, the bus station and its ordered shops. The exits to the east bring the passengers down to the concourse level, into the excitement and activity of mesocity Jerusalem where games of chess, *kebabs* and pirated CDs jostle for attention. This is the space into which the fishermen from Tiberias bring their catch and olives from Nablus are on sale; this is the space where the grapes of Hebron compete with the vineyards of Beer Sheva. Such stations exit at Haifa, Tiberias, Nazareth, Jenin, Nablus, Ramallah, Jerusalem, Bethlehem, Beer Sheva and Gaza.

Sketch of the interior of Jerusalem Station showing the arrival of the train at an upper level, while the mesocity continues to transact its business at the lower level.

Aerial view of Jerusalem. Inset: Early drawings of the underground station showing translucent roofs at ground level. New forms, new beginnings, a break with the past and the absence of orthodoxy.

Two views of the site for the proposed Jerusalem Train Station outside Damascus Gate. It is currently being used as a car park.

Sketch of ramp leading to the concourse of the proposed station from Damascus Gate which has been shown excavated down to its Roman foundations. The ramp penetrates the new glass canopy to gain access to the lower mesocity level.

Earlier version of
Jerusalem
Station's ground-
level atrium
glazing. This
version was
subsequently
revised and can
be seen in the
following chapter.

Section through the station showing the Ottoman walls of Jerusalem in the background and the train arriving at the elevated platform in the foreground.

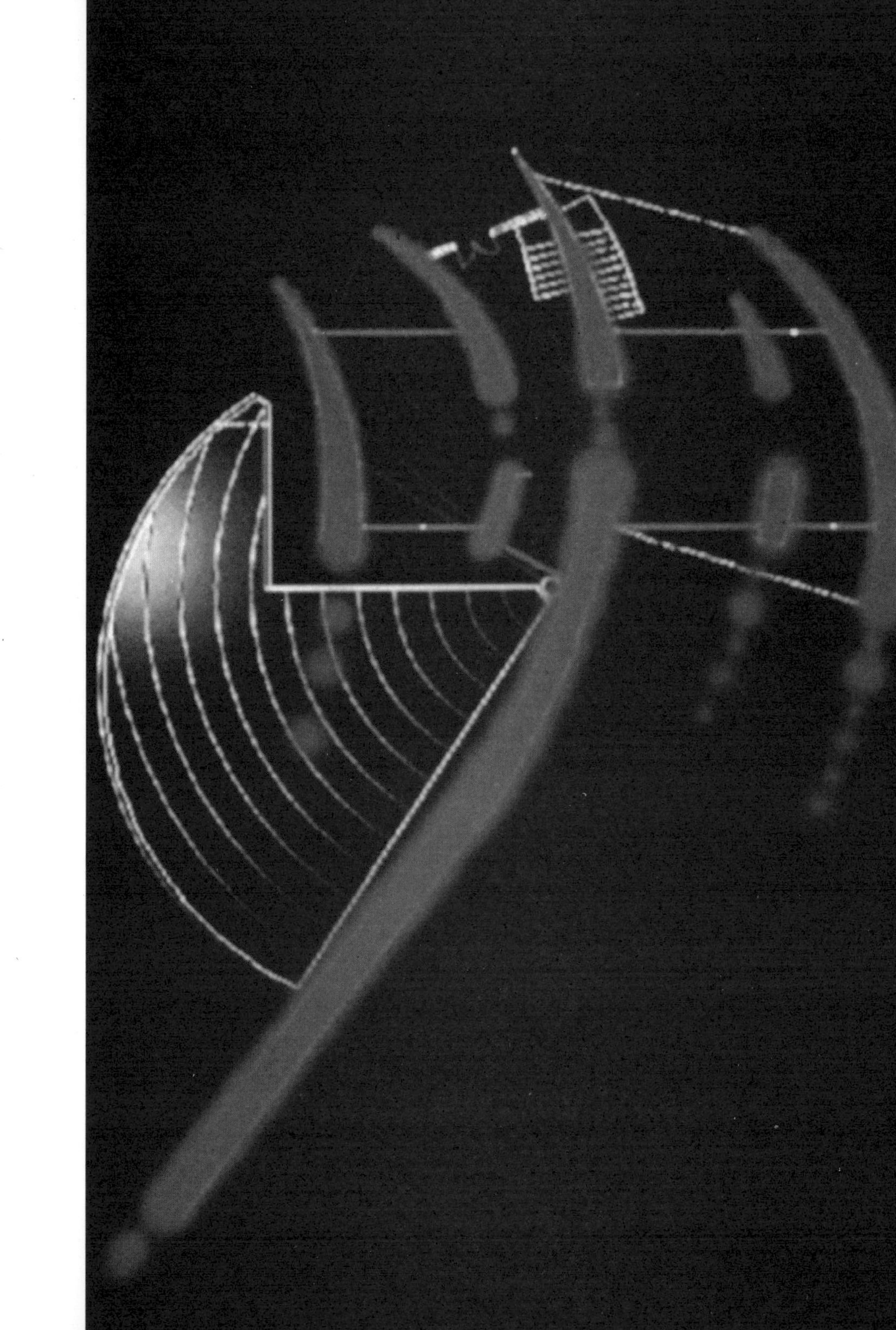

The Long Distant Future

I wish to address two areas from 'the rest of the world' through the design of two proposals, both of which form spaces and situations that are perhaps a little difficult to understand from a position in the west. By the rest of the world I mean, of course, those parts of the globe that cannot reach the plateau where the passing of history has ended and a sense of prosperity, peace and superiority seems to exist as the norm.

The impact of the global free-market economy and the terrible threat of modern war technologies have recently destroyed futures in both Kosovo and Jerusalem. Both are places from the rest of the world, where 100 million people have been thrown into poverty over the last ten years. Under (economic, social and political) conditions far worse than in the 1930s, both places have sought shelter in a past that is simultaneously being quickly reinvented. Both the Kosovars and the Palestinians feel that they have lost their identity and freedom, and hence are suspicious of exponents of the modern world.

At the Anytime conference in Ankara, I spoke about abstract and ancient futures and the extent to which this polarization was beginning to influence architectural ideas across those parts of the globe where ancient futures are being offered as the only viable alternative to the modern world. I argued that in many parts of the world to be modern is increasingly regarded as synonymous with a transatlantic corporate culture – in terms of dress, music, food and language – and something to be avoided and fought at all costs. I have continued to work on this idea, more or less on my own, particularly while spending time in Jerusalem and Kosovo. Until recently, land in both places was appropriated or destroyed by modern weapons originating in the arsenals of the west, as well as in the garage-sales that the erstwhile Soviet republics have been holding to bolster state finances. In Kosovo and in Israel the joysticks of destruction are modern, while the rhetoric of reconstruction is traditional, ancient and often religious. With every calamitous outbreak it is always architecture that is destroyed, and the search for solutions is inevitably monopolized by the military.

My proposals, then, are part of an effort to argue that solutions for reconstruction can be articulated through an architecture that is contemporary and modern; that new civic and secular spaces need not be contested in the same way that religious space is inevitably fought over; that new spaces can be created that are contemporary and relate to futures beyond the ancient; that new types of housing can be built on the foundations of the traditional houses that bombs and bulldozers have flattened.

My own perceptions of the new millennium are based on certain assumptions about the emergence of a new global society, or world order, or whatever else one may like to call it. This new order is demolishing the institutions of previous international structures which were formed in the last century to regulate political and financial affairs, replacing them with alternative constructs that seem to advocate pressurized reconciliation backed by the threat of force. If we assume that the need to demolish those institutions is because they now appear outdated and irrele-vant and did not deliver a promised utopia, then let us agree that the constructs that are being offered as replacements look to create a global society full of new humanism, freedom and democracy. The old, now discarded idea of utopia was critical to the formation of new architectural ideas in the early part of the twentieth century. Indeed, utopia was to a certain extent given form by that new architecture. My proposals, then, are a sort of heroic attempt at exploring some ideas about how architecture can respond to the newly-emerging reality in the absence of a utopian agenda.

Beginning 21 March 1999, the United States-led NATO forces launched cruise missile and bomb attacks at targets across the Federal Republic of Yugoslavia. Within 78 days, as a consequence of the retaliations to this attack, large parts of Kosovo were bombed and bulldozed into rubble. Half the housing-stock was destroyed, the electrical infrastructure was completely devastated, and the agricultural system seriously damaged. I was sent to Kosovo by the United Nations to propose a national housing reconstruction strategy. The architectural proposal focuses a site in the village of

NATO forces launched at Serbia Yugoslavia in March 1999 and went on to launch at Afghanistan in 2001.

Office building in Central Prestina, Kosovo's capital city, destroyed by the Serbs.

Kosovo.
Above:
The destroyed village of Chabra.
Below:
Japanese donors rush to help.

Kosovo. Destruction of a church for a mosque. An eye for an eye.

children
on the edge
Mobile Hygiene Unit

Kosovo.
Above:
The collapse of the industrial sector.
Below:
Body Shop provides mobile toilets in the destroyed villages.

Potential building material for reconstructing houses lies in a rubble – rubble left behind by bulldozers and bombs.

The rubble is packed into wire-cage gabions which are used as the basic material for the walls of houses.

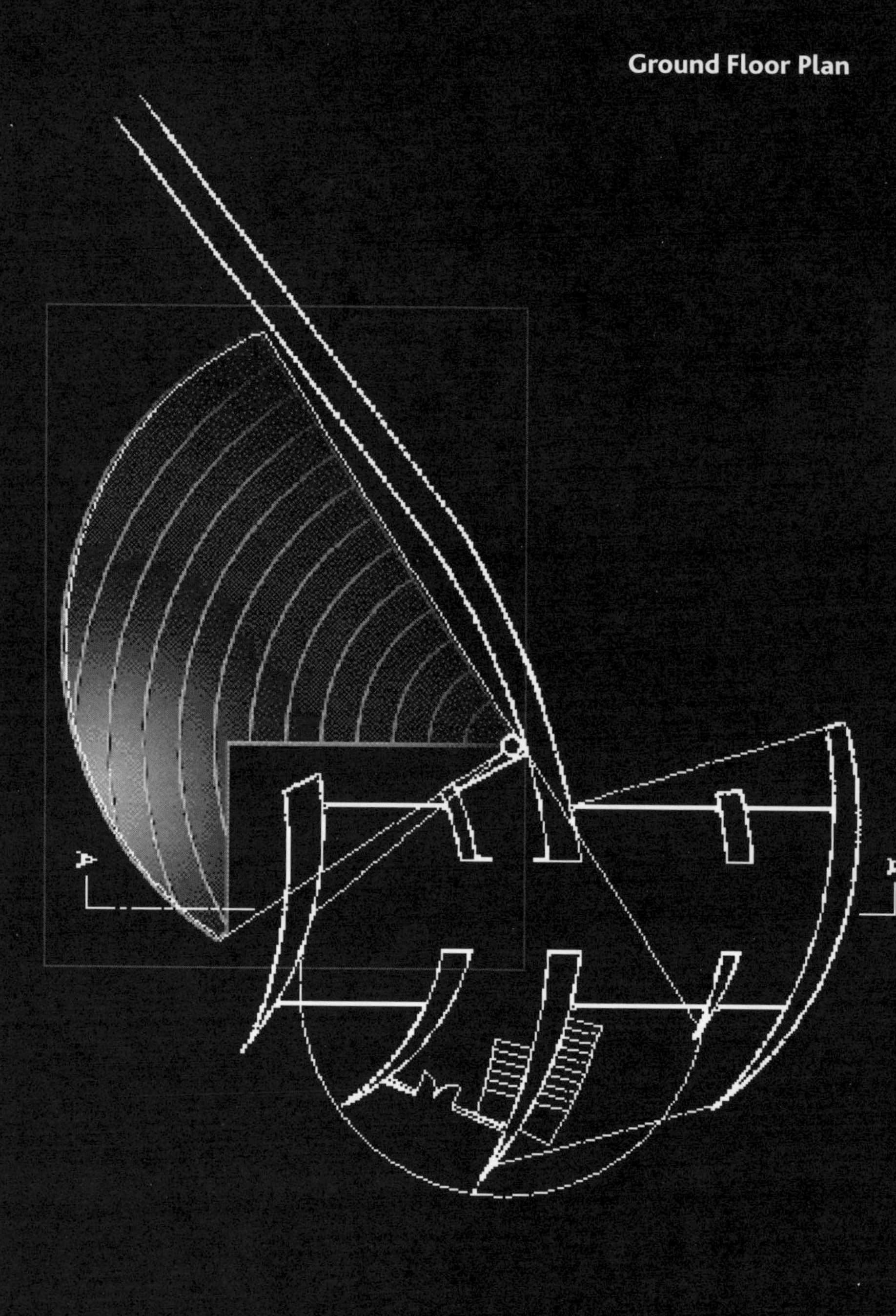

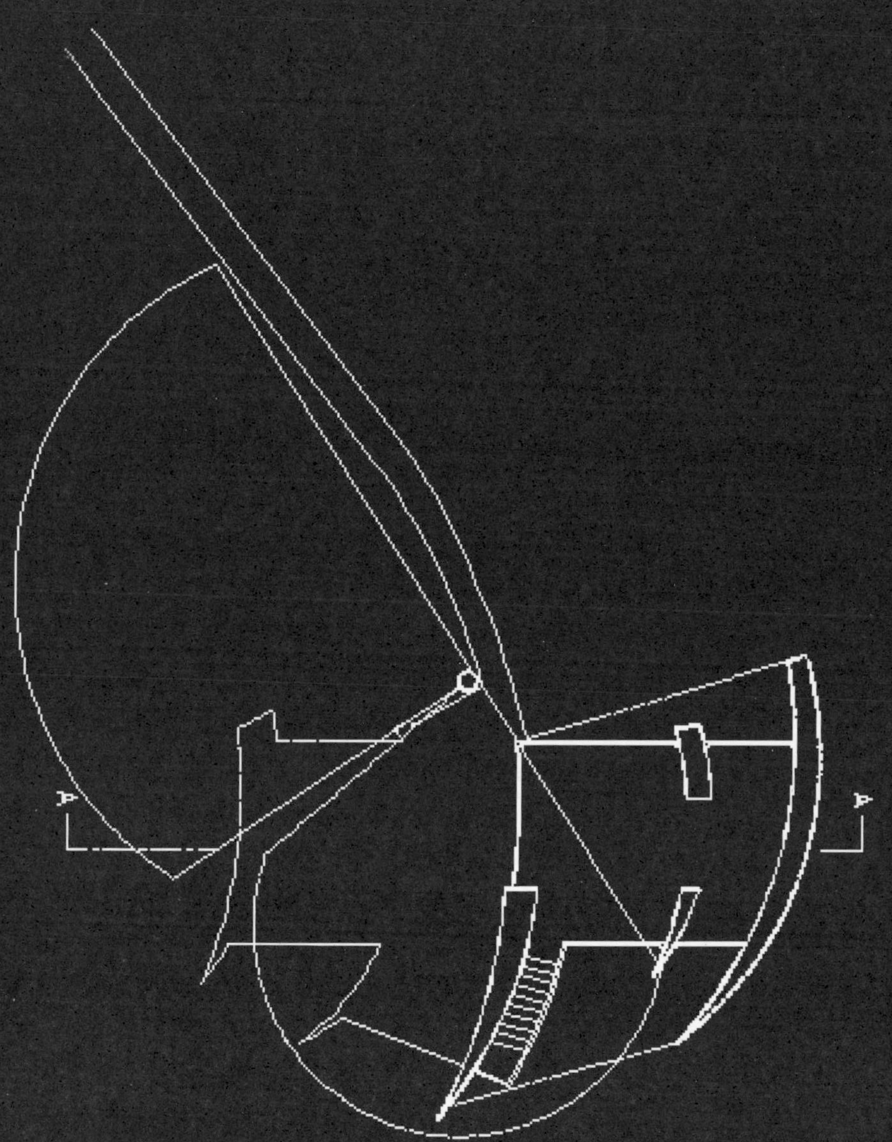

Plans of ground floor and roof of houses in Kosovo. Walls are constructed with gabions filled with the rubble of destroyed houses. The long tail is the ramp up which the Kosovars can haul building materials in barrows, avoiding the use of scaffolding, which is unavailable.

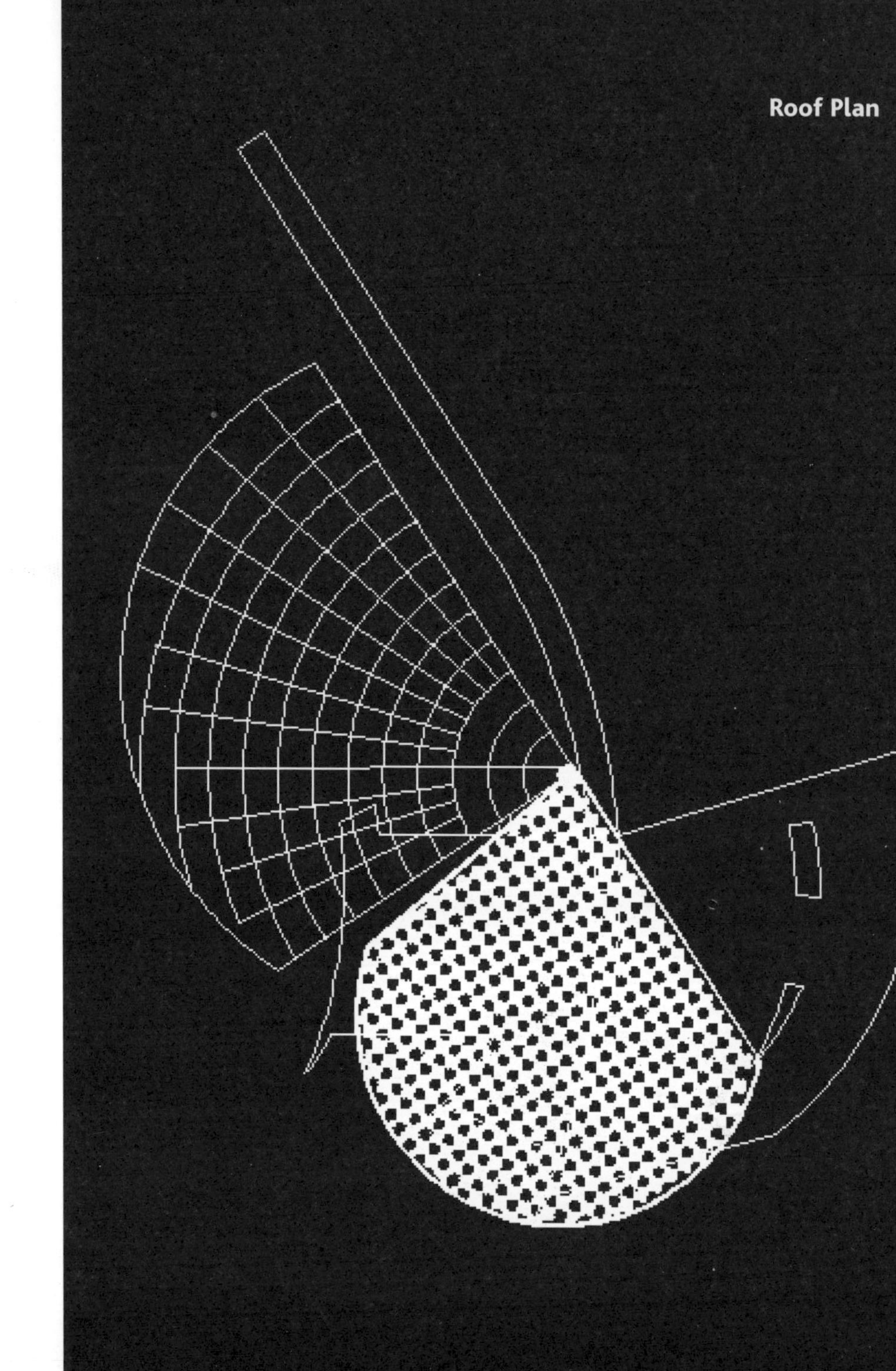

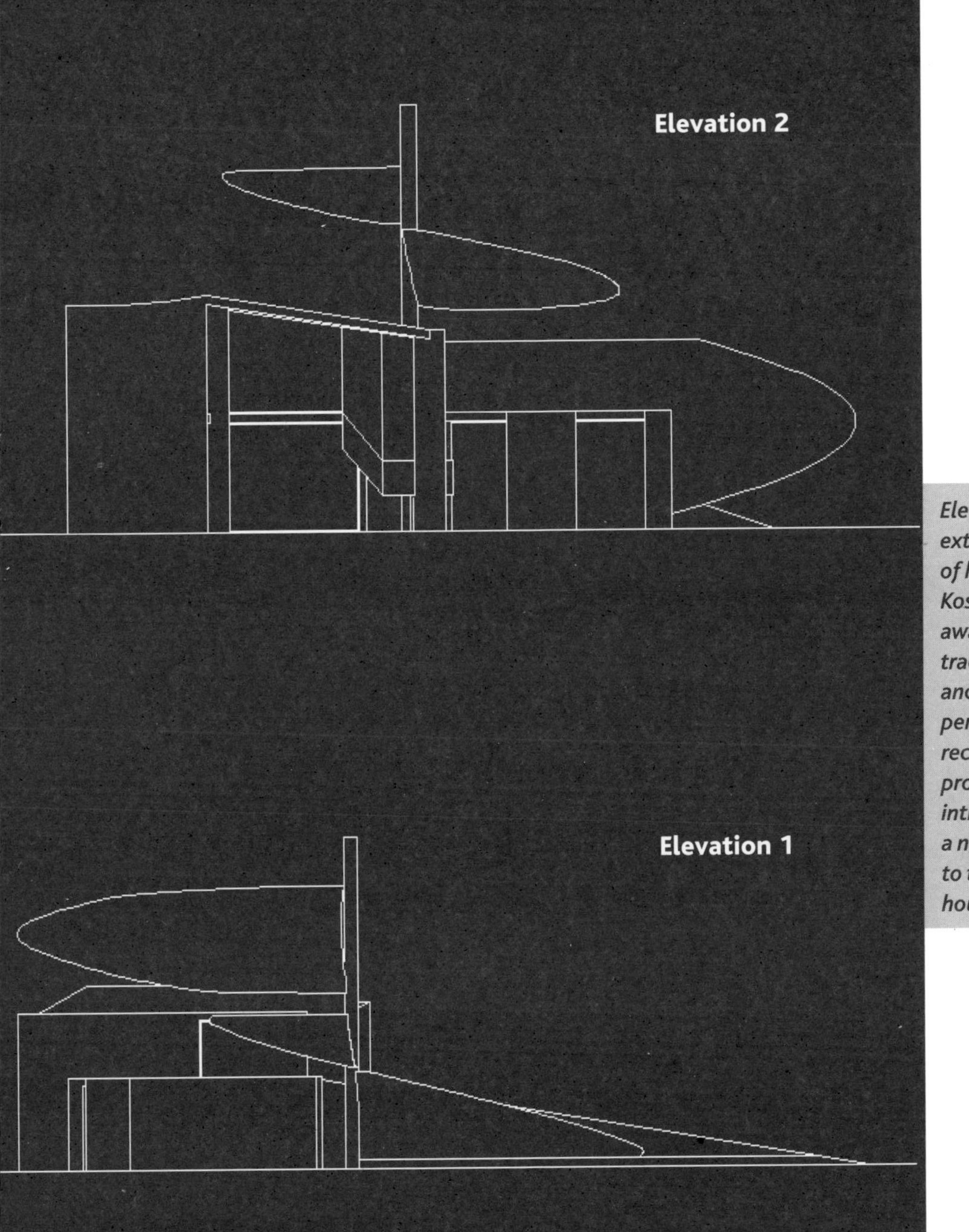

Elevations and external image of houses in Kosovo. Moving away from traditional images and memories of period houses, the reconstruction process introduces a new aesthetic to the village house.

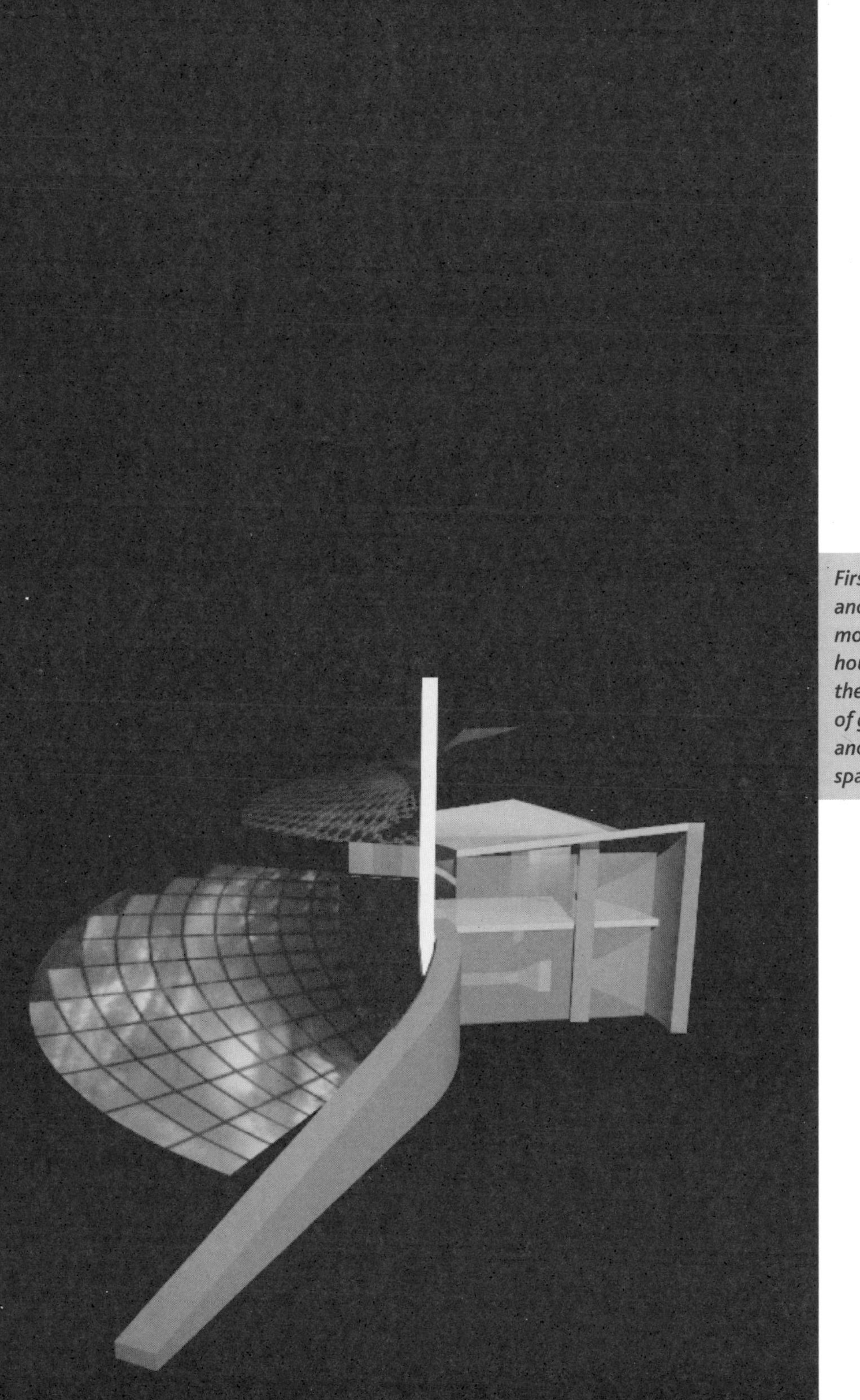

First-floor plan and views of the model of a Kosovo house, explaining the construction of gabion walls and internal spaces.

Chabra where not a single house was left standing. The only affordable and available building material was the rubble of former structures. So, for the reconstruction project, this rubble was packed into metal gabions to form the walls of the new houses, emblematically combining the reality and the metaphor of the crisis there. In addition to the walls, the only other elements of the new houses in Chabra are a series of donated solar panels to provide electricity, and a glass house for growing essential foods during the snows of winter.

At the site of my second proposal, Jerusalem, it became clear to me that there are, in many ways, two cites. The old city, enclosed within ancient walls, belongs to the Arabs, while the new Jerusalem belongs to Israel. Between the two cities lies a blurred space – a buffer-zone – in which both communities hesitate to implement radical change. If either of them actually initiated anything a riot would ensue, because such movement would cause a shift in the imagined lines of control, with one of the two contenders emerging as a victorious claimant to the whole of Jerusalem. The Ottoman walls neatly define the boundaries of old Jerusalem. New Jerusalem is well settled around a new city-centre full of boutiques and extending into endless suburbs that are constantly expanding as the Jewish population grows larger than the Arab one within the city limits.

The site for the proposal is in the fuzzy zone. Within the buffer between the two cities lies a square-shaped site that separates the tense outer edges of the old and the new cities, and is currently used as a car park. New Jerusalem is a macrocity of literati where the civic order of Zion has been codified into a series of written rules and regulations. Inevitably, as in all macrourban cultures, these rules resist the pressures of emergent, everchanging relationships and initiatives arising from the collaborations and negotiations of citizens interacting with and adjusting to each other. These actively enforced municipal regulations resist the dynamics that convert folk cultures into urban civilizations. The Arab city, on the other hand, is a mesocity of intellectuals, of spoken cultures – a city that is reluctant to codify its civic order into written rules and regulations. Meso is derived from the Greek word 'mesos', meaning 'middle'. I have coined the word mesocity to signify a city of temporary stability, mediating its spaces and forms between the pressures of the microworld of citizens and the macrocity world of civic order, written rules and regulations, and the imposition of state law on the city's regulatory orders. Here the community meshes its activities not along functional regulations but on the basis of a permissiveness bordering on the turbulence of a moving stream, where tolerance and acceptability of the ensuing chaos is almost an asset to use and exploit in new ways. As the unfortunate jewel that has to be shared between Muslims, Jews and Christians, the old city becomes the battleground where the orthodox in each community fight for it to become their own.

The project proposes Jerusalem as one of ten stations strung along a new rail-link, stretching from Haifa to Nazareth, Jenin, Nablus, Ramallah, Jerusalem, Bethlehem, Beer Sheva and Gaza. The train moves across the physical and ideological barriers that both sides have imposed. It is about connectivity of the economy and its people, and about new markets and choices. It is a train for commuters, and for goods and services. Equally significantly, the rail-bed forms a new nationwide water-carrier which will be able to bring water from the desalination plants of Haifa, the Sea of Galilee and the aquifers under the West Bank, to be distributed to the dry agricultural terraces of the West Bank in Palestine and the deserts of the Negev in Israel. The track and the water-carrier are integrated. The train rides, so to speak, on the tube carrying the water. Each of the ten stations on the route provides a civic concourse for economic and social exchange.

Jerusalem Station represents a kind of celebratory architecture that could provide alternative humane solutions to the hastily-sketched military response to a divided city. This contention is based on my own refusal to accept the viability of a separate Palestine and Israel. My proposal assumes the gradual integration of both these parts as the only viable alternative to the disastrous consequence of setting up two conflicting Lilliputian nations.

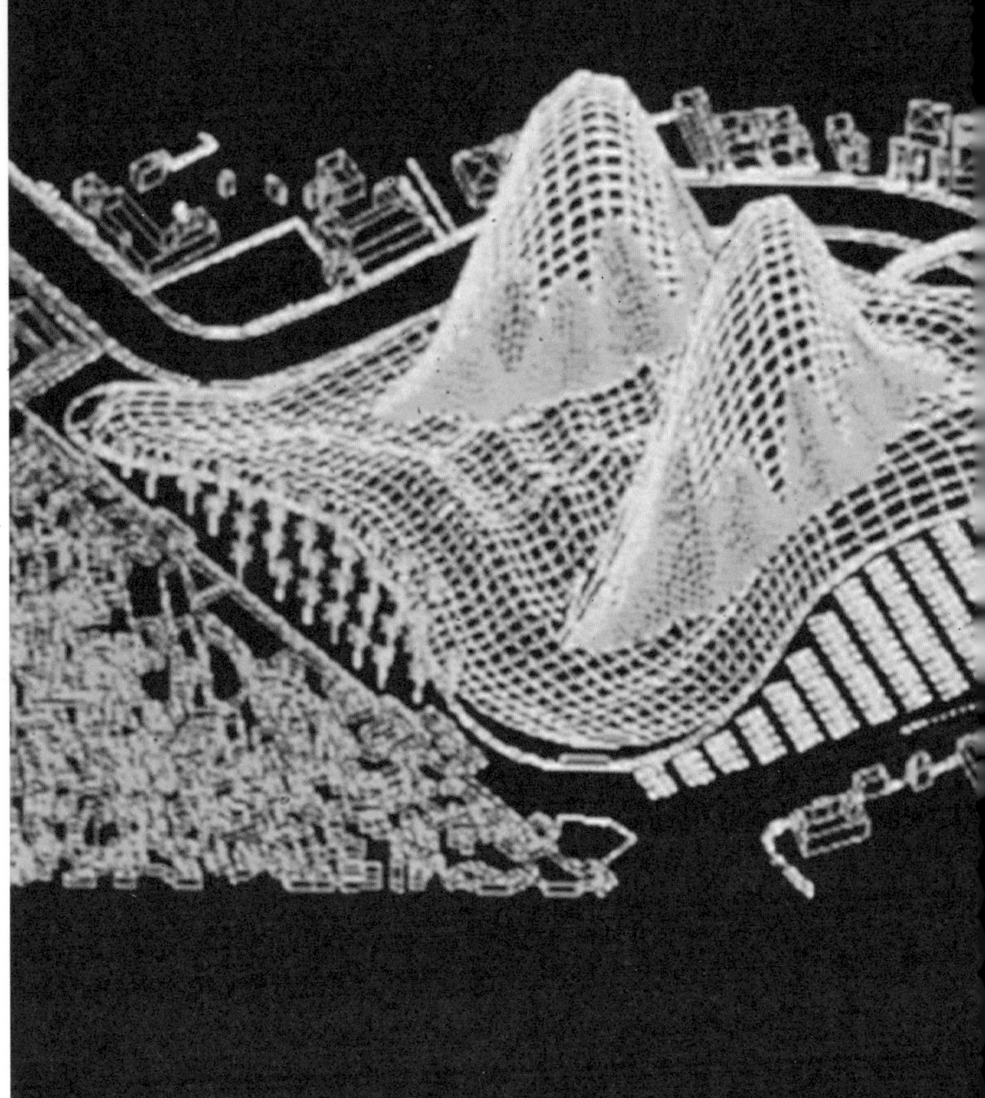

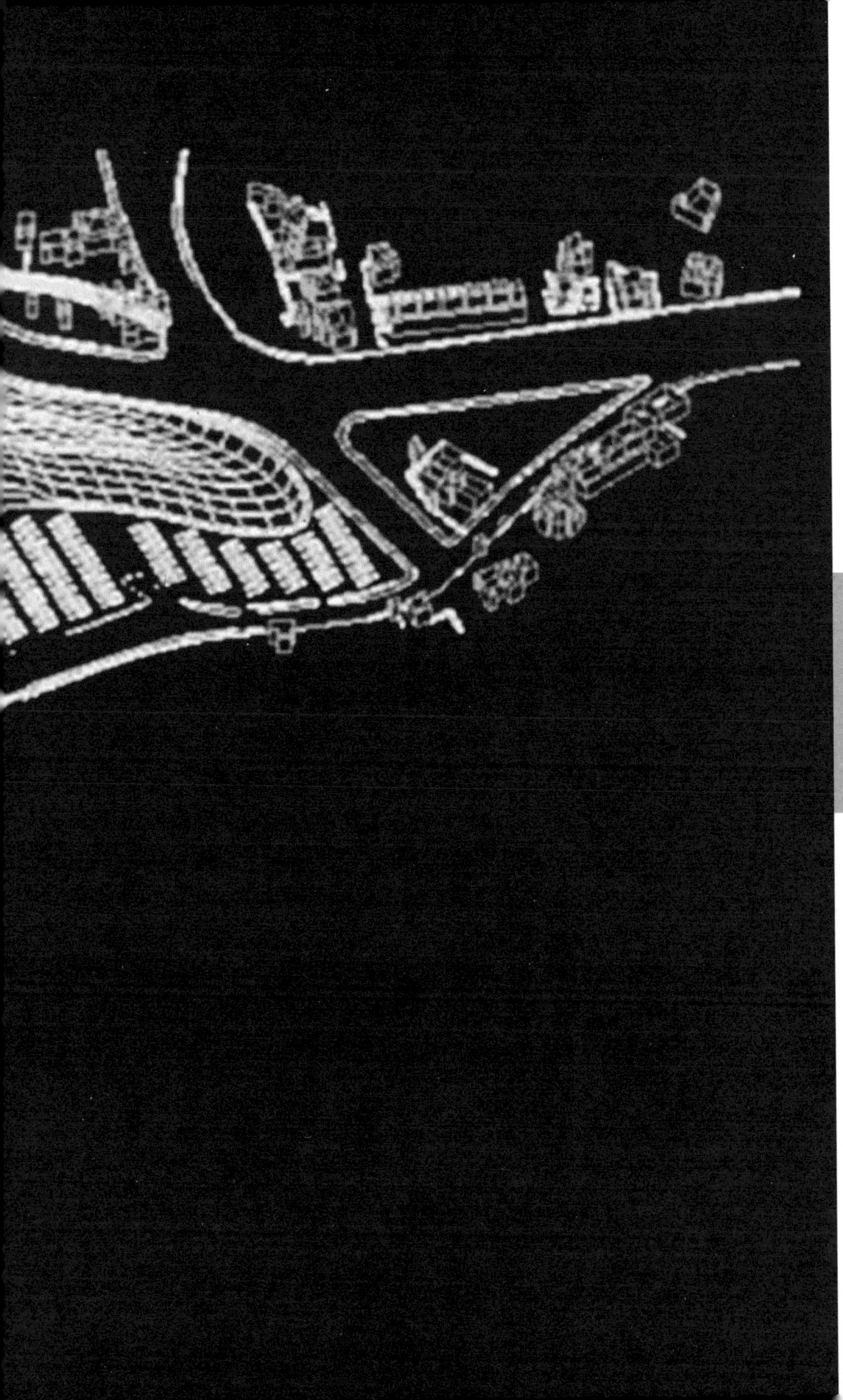

View of revised proposal for Jerusalem Station showing the changes envisaged in the roof cover of the concourse space.

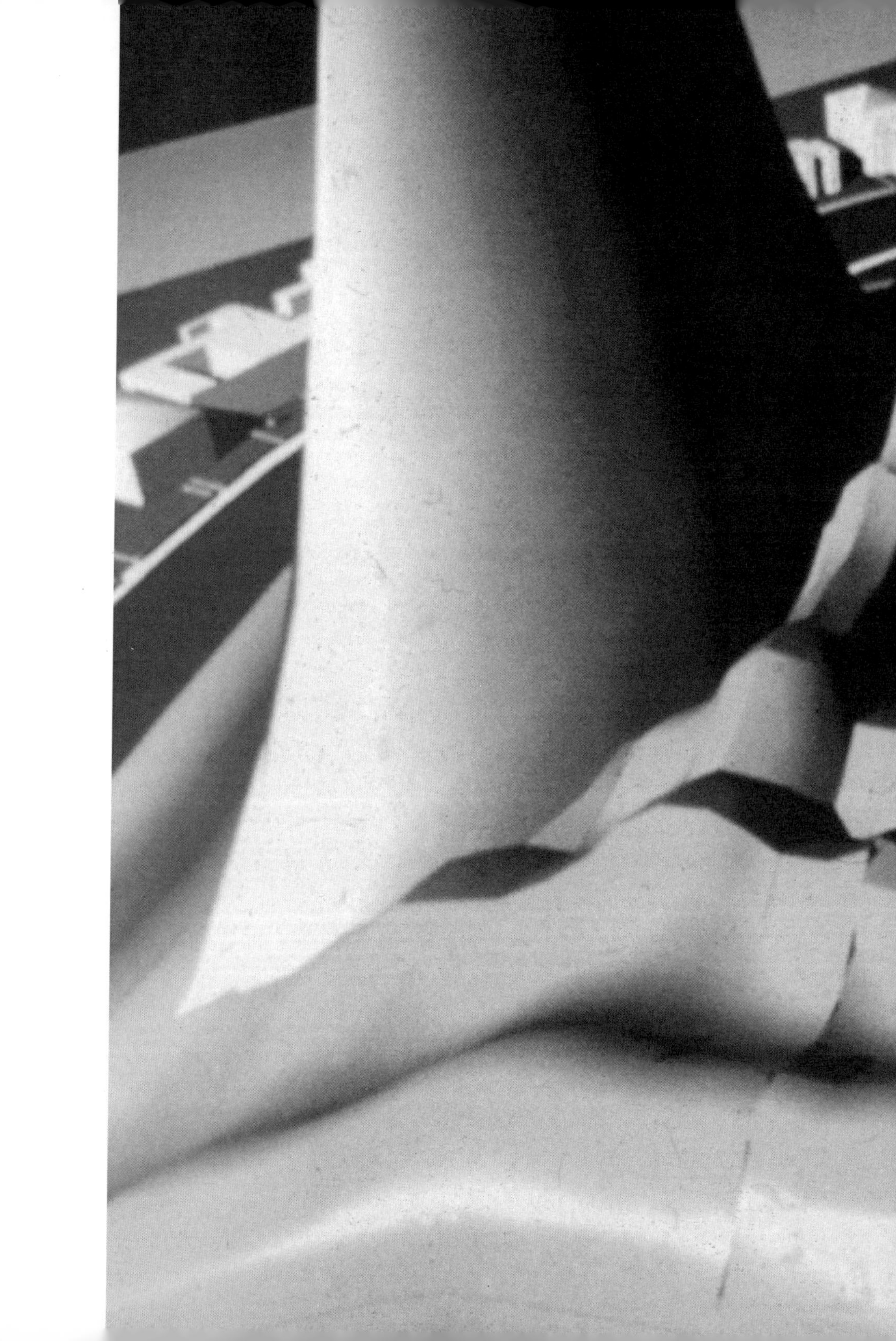

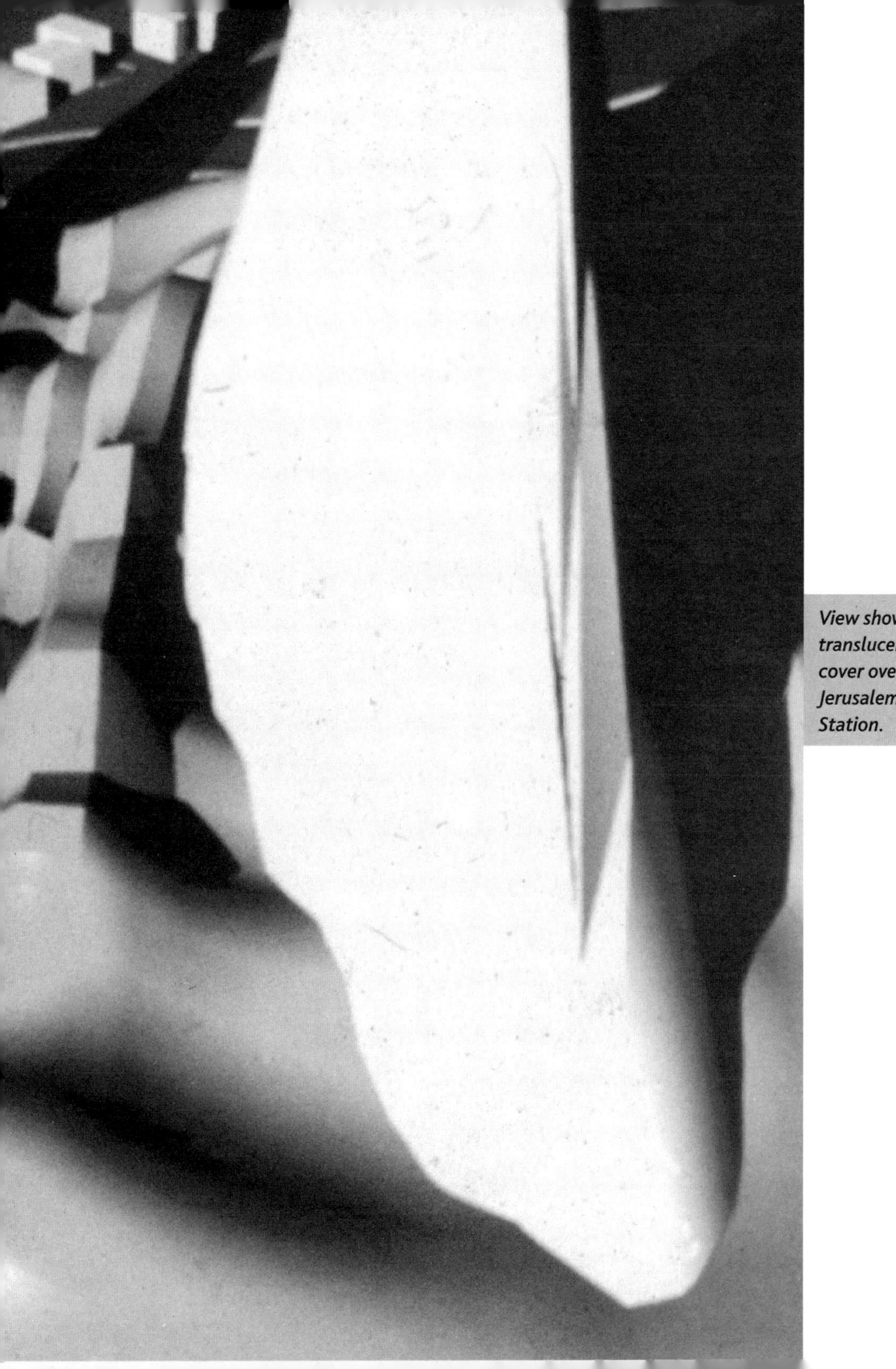

*View showing
translucent roof
cover over
Jerusalem
Station.*

The extent of *Jerusalem Station* on the surface.

Plan of proposed station at Jerusalem. The train winds through the concourse at a raised level. Sloping ramps bring the passengers to the mesocity.

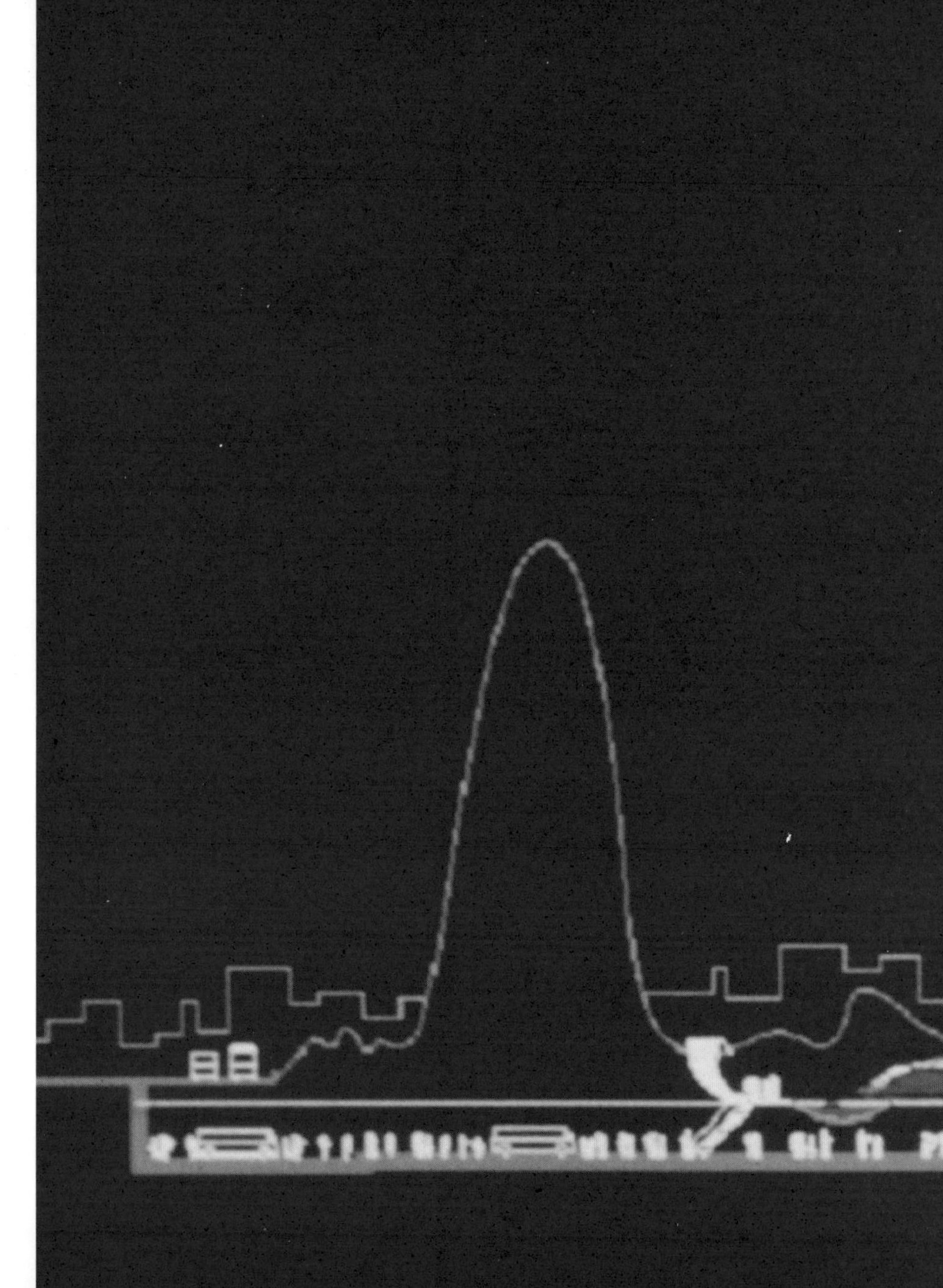

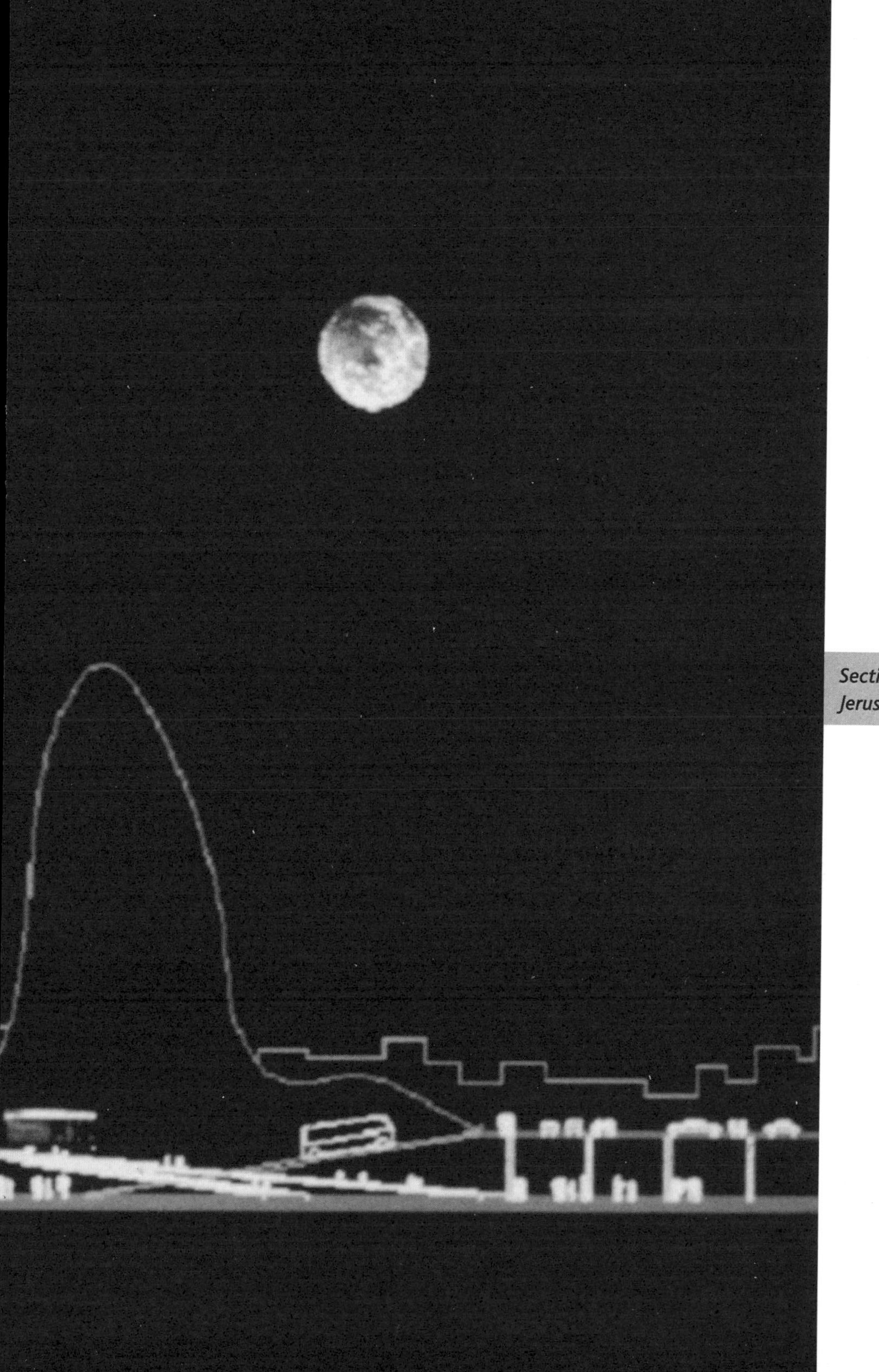

Section through Jerusalem Station.

Notes

'Abstract & Ancient Futures' was first published in *Anytime,* edited by Cynthia C. Davidson, Anyone Corporation, New York, and MIT Press, Cambridge, Mass., 1999.

'Countermodernism' was first published as 'The Persistence of Pre-Modernism', in *Contemporary Architecture and City Form: The South Asian Paradigm,* edited by Farooq Ameen, Marg Publications, Mumbai, 1997.

'Awarding Architecture' was first published as 'The Conscience of Architecture', in *Legacies for the Future: Contemporary Architecture in Islamic Societies,* Thames and Hudson, London, and The Aga Khan Award for Architecture, 1998.

'The Long Distant Future' was originally published as 'The Loneliness of the Long Distant Future', in *Anything,* edited by Cynthia C. Davidson, Anyone Corporation, New York, and MIT Press, Cambridge, Mass., 2001.

Acknowledgements

The opening and closing chapters of this book were written in response to invitations from Cynthia Davidson, who edited them for publication in the ANY volumes. Suha Ozkan encouraged me to access the archives of the Aga Khan Award for Architecture and obtain images which are reproduced here. It is difficult to repay him fully for the valuable advice and comments he made when I discussed so many ideas with him about the nature of contemporary times.

For the chapter on 'The New Canaanites', I was fortunate to get the help of some masters who guided me through the abnormal conditions that persisted in the civilization of the Levant at the close of the last century. I was able to visit the nooks and corners of Palestine with officials and architects of the Ministry of Education, and I would like to thank Fawaz Mujahid, Hanan Yesin, Faten, Gergana Elzeer and Suzy. Amira Hass took me to places outside the Palestinian Authority to meet Israelis whom I would never have been able to meet on my own. As my neighbour, she became a real guide. Glen Bowman's insights and experiences of Palestine and Israel brought me closer to the deeper levels of this region. George Hinditalyan, an Armenian scholar, introduced me to Christian Jerusalem, its stones, ancient and modern graffiti and the teashops. I had innumerable discussions with him in the lanes of Jerusalem, which gave me a new understanding about the city. Suad Aamiry brought me down to the earth and introduced me to the architecture of Palestine. Sadia Touqan showed me how she practised the gentle art of architectural restoration under the sounds of the heavy breathing of Israeli soldiers who dogged her projects deep inside the Kasbah of Jerusalem. The late Awad Islam guided me through the Haram Sharif; Khalid Quawasme took me through the restored streets of Hebron, dodging through barbed-wire fences that obscure the route to Abraham's Tomb. Veronique Dauge at the UNESCO office in Ramallah introduced me to the archaeology of the Levant. As a neighbour and my project director, she spent countless hours talking about the various sites in the region. Kalpana, my wife, joined me for some months in Palestine and Israel and did a series of watercolours. Two of these I have used to overdraw the proposed train. Rebecca Sternberg visited me in Jerusalem, gave me a number of references and showed me around Tel Aviv. She also obtained for me satellite imagery of the Levant and Jerusalem. I am indebted to Michael Sorkin for putting me in touch with her. Moshe Safdie provided me with drawings of the site outside Damascus Gate which were used by Harvard students in their proposals, and also took me to see some of his work. Through his eyes I was able to understand many Israeli concerns and hopes about Jerusalem.

My innumerable visits to the Balkans were made possible through the UNDP offices in Bulgaria, Romania and Kosovo. All these visits were facilitated by Antonio Vigilante, the Resident Representative in Sofia. His trust and faith in my ability to go into the interiors of this region and conduct my research without any prompting enabled me to make independent observations and proposals to the UN. During my missions to Bulgaria and Romania I was helped beyond measure by Clarice Strauss, the Project Director of my programme in Sofia. Her intense sympathy towards the deprived and her commitment to help them enabled it to succeed as a model programme for social support in the Balkans.

The potential for publishing all this material as a book was seen by Rajen Prasad and Indu Chandrasekhar, who provided me great encouragement during my efforts to assemble all the material and images. Purnima Joshi sat with me for many hours battling with the design and layout of the book, and Ram Rahman and Rashmi Kalecka provided crucial inputs for the final design.

Credits

Cover From *The Flights of Icarus* by Donald Lehmkuhl (Paper Tiger, United
Kingdom, 1977)

Endpapers 'Soap bubbles in steel frame' by Romi Khosla, photographs by Barry Melor

1, 9 From 'Ultimate City – the last city on earth' by Romi Khosla

20–21 From *El Croquis* by Frank Ghery, 1991–95

21 inset Plan from Mayapur Master Plan team

22 above Image of a possible future by Bruce Pennington

22 below View of the World Trade Center on 11 September 2001

27 above Axonometric drawing from *El Croquis* by Frank Ghery, 1991–95

27 below Drawing of Temple of Vedic Planetarium by Keith Critchlow

29 above Plan of Spa Tokay from *Wiggle* by Michael Sorkin (The Monacelli Press
Inc., New York, 1998)

29 below Layout model of Mayapur temple city, photograph by Romi Khosla

31 From brochure of the National Religion Bureau of China

32 above Photograph by Romi Khosla

32 below Model of temple by Mayapur Master Plan Team

33 Commercially available photograph

34, 35 above & below Images of Frankfurt from postcards bought in the street

37 Image from Maitreya Temple Project brochure

39 above From *My Land and My People* by The Dalai Lama (Panther, 1964),
photograph by Tolstoy and Dolan

39 below Photograph by Romi Khosla

40 Photograph by Fosco Moriani

41, 42 Photographs by Romi Khosla

45 above Photograph from Samarkand Chief Architect's Office, courtesy Nematjan
Saditov

45 middle & below Photographs by Romi Khosla

46 Drawing by Romi Khosla

46 inset From *Timurid Architecture of Iran and Turan*, Vol. II, by Lisa Golombek and
Donald Wilber (Princeton, 1988), drawing by K. Herdig

47 above & below Photographs by Romi Khosla

50 left Photographs by Romi Khosla

50 right Photographs by Vladimir Sis and Jan Vanis

51, 52, 53 Photographs by Romi Khosla

55 above & below Photographs courtesy Aga Khan Award for Architecture

56 above & below Photographs by Romi Khosla

57 above Photograph by Romi Khosla

57 below Drawing by Neil Gutschow and Gotz Hagmuller, Kathmandu, photograph by Romi Khosla

58 Photograph by Romi Khosla

66 above & below, 68 above Photographs courtesy Aga Khan Award for Architecture

68 below Drawing by Tony Garnier

69 Photograph by Romi Khosla

74 above & below, 75, 76–77, 78 above & below, 79 above & below, 80 above & below Photographs courtesy Aga Khan Award for Architecture

83 Drawing by Romi Khosla

88–89 From *Tabo: A lamp for the kingdom* by Deborah E. Klimburg-Salter (Skira Editore, Milan, 1997), photograph by Jaroslav Poncar

90 From *The Sacred Art of Tibet*, catalogue of exhibition (Royal Academy of Art, London, 1992)

93 above & below From *Tower of David: Where Jerusalem Begins,* catalogue of exhibition (The Jerusalem Foundation, 1999)

98, 99 Drawings by Romi Khosla

102 Photomontage by Ganesh. Photograph of Jerusalem from the Hill of Olives by Romi Khosla, fire images from Bruce Pennington (Paper Tiger, United Kingdom, 1976)

104–105 Watercolour by Kalpana Sahni

106–107 above & below Photographs by Romi Khosla

109 Site Plan courtesy Moshe Safdie

110–111 Photograph by Romi Khosla

116 Courtesy Palestinian Exploration Fund, London

117 Postcards of lithographs by David Roberts

120 Commercially available postcards

122–123 above Commercially available postcard

122 below Photograph by Romi Khosla

123 below Photograph by Romi Khosla

127 From *Canaanites: The People of the Past* by Jonathan Tubb (The British Museum Press, London, 1998)

129 From *Jerusalem: Arab Origins and Heritage*, M.A. Aamiry (Longmans, 1978)

134–135 Photograph from Elia Photo Service, Jerusalem

138–139 From *Canaanites: The People of the Past* by Jonathan Tubb (The British Museum Press, London, 1998)

CREDITS

148, 153 Maps from Palestinian National Authority

150 Photograph by Romi Khosla

156–157 Photograph from photo service, Jerusalem

159 above Photograph by Romi Khosla

159 below Commercially available postcard

160–161 above & below Photographs by Romi Khosla

164–165 above, middle & below Photographs by Romi Khosla

168–169, 179 below Photographs from *Israeli Obstacles to Economic Development in the Occupied Territories* (Jerusalem Media and Communication Centre, 1994)

172 Maps from Palestinian National Authority

173 Census data from Palestinian National Authority, Central Bureau of Statistics

176–177. Commercially available map

179 above Census data from Palestinian National Authority, Central Bureau of Statistics

182–183 above & below Photographs by Romi Khosla

182 inset Postcard of Sistine Chapel

185 above & below Postcards, commercially available

187 above & below Photograph from Elia Photo Service, Jerusalem

190 Drawing by Romi Khosla

191 Commercially available satellite image with train route superimposed

176, 181, 182, 183 Drawings by Romi Khosla

196–197 above & below Photographs by Romi Khosla

201 Drawing by Romi Khosla

202–203 Commercially available photograph of Jerusalem

203 inset Drawing by Romi Khosla

204–205 Photographs by Romi Khosla

206, 207, 208–209, 210 Drawings by Romi Khosla

214 Image from aircraft magazine

215, 216–217 above & below, 218–219 above & below, 220–221 above & below, 222 Photographs by Romi Khosla

223 Image from Italian gabion company catalogue

224–29 Drawings by Romi Khosla

232–233, 234–235, 236–237, 238–239, 240–241 Drawings by Romi Khosla

Published by Tulika Books
35A/1 (third floor)
Shahpur Jat
New Delhi 110 049
India

© Romi Khosla 2002

First published in India 2002

ISBN 81-85229-55-4

Designed by Ram Rahman,
Rashmi Kalecka and Romi Khosla,
typeset at Tulika Print Communication
Services, New Delhi, and printed at
Baba Barkha Nath Printers, Najafgarh
Road Industrial Area, Delhi.